DEDICATION

This book is dedicated to the memory of my father,
Rev. Wm. E. Mittendorf, a great man.

Applying Inspiring Biographies from the Bible for Personal Growth: Examining Faith, Optimism, Forgiveness, Courage and Perseverance (Book One)

Kimberly Mittendorf Hensley, MA, MEd

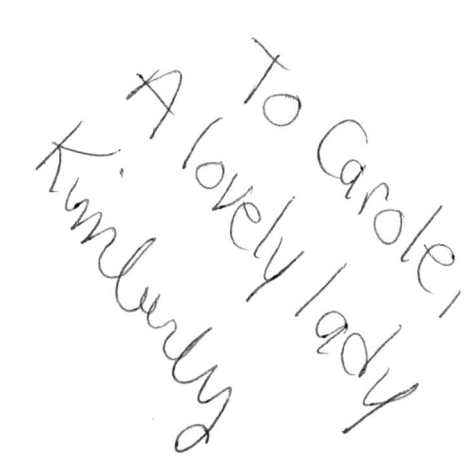

Copyright © 2015 Kimberly Mittendorf Hensley

All rights reserved.

ISBN-10: 1514-800640
ISBN-13: 978-151480064

CONTENTS

1. Their Stories Can Inform Your Story   1
2. Faith: Believing Every Promise for Your Life   7
3. Optimism: Yes We Can!   19
4. Forgiveness: Let Go and Be Free   29
5. Courage: I Come to You in the Name of the Lord   39
6. Perseverance: Never Give Up   57
7. What Will Your Story Be?   69
    Endnotes   77
    About the Author   87

Unless otherwise indicated, all Scriptures are taken from *The Living Bible*, ©1971 owned by assignment by Illinois Regional Bank N.A. (as trustee). Used by permission of Tyndale House Publishers, Inc., Wheaton, Illinois 60189. All rights reserved.

Scripture references marked MESSAGE are taken from *The Message Bible* © 1993 by Eugene N. Peterson, NavPress, PO Box 35001, Colorado Springs, Co 80935, 4th printing in USA 1-994. Published in association with the literary agency – Alive Comm. PO Box 49068, Colorado Springs, CO 80949. Used by permission.

Scripture references marked NKJV are taken from the *New King James Version*, © 1979, 1980, 1982 by Thomas Nelson, Inc., Publishers Used by permission.

Scripture references marked AMP are taken from *The Amplified Bible, Old Testament,* © 1965 and 1987 by the Zondervan Corporation, and from *The Amplified New Testament,* ©1954, 1958, 1987 by the Lockman Foundation. Used by permission.

Scripture references marked KJV are taken from the *King James Version* of the Bible.

Also used The Life Recovery Bible and The Archeological Study Bible

Dear reader,

You would help me greatly by reviewing this book on Amazon.com. Thank you for your support.

I would love to hear from you. My email address is khensley@zoomtown.com. My website is www.supportbykim.com which also promotes my Christian coaching business for people with disabilities and their caregivers.

Blessings,

Kimberly Mittendorf Hensley, Amelia, Ohio, November, 2015

1 THEIR STORY CAN INFORM YOUR STORY

By examining and applying the stories of Biblical characters to your own life, you can grow and mature in a myriad of amazing ways. The Bible is a sacred book of meaning and purpose and the stories within its covers have eternal and astounding implications. This study will look specifically at the faith of Abraham, the optimism of Joshua and Caleb, the forgiveness of Joseph, the courage of David and the perseverance of Nehemiah. Its purpose is to help you develop such strengths of your own.

These ancient stories are meant to inspire you in your day to day walk with the Lord. Personal growth is not only one of the most important attributes you can pursue, it can also bring great joy and satisfaction to your life. Whether riding on a camel beside Abraham, scoping out the Promised Land with Joshua and Caleb, organizing the prison with Joseph, hiding in the caves with David, or bricklaying with Nehemiah, these adventures have many truths to reveal.

Faith is a great attribute with which to open a book. As Hebrews 11:1-2 teaches, "Faith is the confidence that what we hope for will actually happen; it gives us assurance about things we cannot see. Through their faith, the people in the days of old earned a good reputation."

Do you have confidence that what you hope for will really occur? Do you have assurance even if things in the natural don't look so promising?

Abraham was a man from the days of old who followed God with great trust and abandon. He had a wonderful capacity to believe God completely and this helped him create a life that honored the Lord. Abraham did not try to live by his own effort. Rather, he freely admitted his total dependence on his Maker.

We have something of infinite value that Abraham did not have. It is the Bible, God's infallible Word. When we know the Word, we know God's heart. As Abraham had intimate communion with God, we can have that same knowledge of the Creator through His Word.

Through belief in the Word Incarnate, Jesus, we become the spiritual descendants of Abraham. Chapter two will explore the story of Abraham to help us make more sense of our own lives and give us lessons in faithful devotion to the Lord.

Abraham left everything he knew to follow God without knowing where he was going. He trusted God for a son after he and his wife were well beyond childbearing age. Later, he was willing to sacrifice his beloved son, Isaac, when God required it.

But at the last moment God declared to Abraham: "Lay down the knife; don't hurt the lad in any way for I know that God is first in your life – you have not withheld even your beloved son from me." (Genesis 22: 12)

Although God saved Abraham's dear son, many years later He allowed His own beloved Son to be sacrificed for you and for me so that we could live forever with Him in eternity.

Because of what Christ did on our behalf, a poor performance cannot strike us out of God's plan. Can you even imagine the wonders God has stored up for you if you will demonstrate great faith as Abraham did?

Chapter three explores optimism; specifically that of Joshua and Caleb. Optimism can be defined as the belief that good ultimately prevails over evil. It can also be seen as the tendency to take the most hopeful view of a matter.[1]

Certainly Joshua and Caleb embodied this definition of optimism as they looked upon the Promised Land. When asked if the Israelis could take the land, they responded with a resounding, "Yes, we can!"

As two of the twelve spies who went into the land "flowing with milk and honey," Joshua and Caleb saw the resident Anakim giants but were not intimidated by them. As they stood before Moses, Caleb exclaimed, "Let us go up at once and possess it, for we are well able to conquer it." (Numbers 13:30)

How do you respond when observing your personal Anakim giants? Can you show the optimism of Caleb and Joshua?

Optimism is encouraging and empowering. It can help you set goals for your life. It can inspire you to move forward on the cherished dreams you hold deep within your most essential self.

God gives you those dreams that you carry in your heart. He has a good plan for your life. As He sent challenging situations into Joshua and Caleb's lives, He will send such situations into your life. To live your most productive and fulfilling life, you must have the optimism to embrace the challenges He sends your way.

Chapter four focuses on forgiveness. If you want to experience joy in your life, forgive someone. Each time you forgive a deep hurt, you give yourself a new beginning. Most importantly, because Jesus shed His blood for our sins, we can be completely forgiven by God.

Through forgiveness, we can clear away toxic emotions such as anger, disgust, and guilt. Whether we release such destructive feelings toward ourselves or others, there is real freedom and healing in the act of forgiving.

All of us need both to forgive and be forgiven. We have all sinned. First John 1:8-10 contains a beautiful promise we can hold on to: "If we say that we have no sin, we are only fooling ourselves and refusing to accept the truth. But if we confess our sins to Him, He can be depended upon to forgive us and to cleanse us from every wrong."

I don't know about you, but these words give me a lot of peace. Jesus is the same yesterday, today, and forever and He is willing to forgive all past, present and future sins. Wow. That is really Good News.

A Biblical example of a person who exhibited great forgiveness is Joseph. His story is told in Genesis. Joseph went through so much unfairness in his life. He was sold into slavery by his brothers, jailed for something he did not do, and left to languish for years in prison without reason.

Yet everywhere he went, he kept rising to leadership positions. Finally, he was called before Pharaoh to interpret dreams. He did so successfully and eventually became second-in-command in Egypt. When his brothers came to Egypt needy and hungry, Joseph chose to forgive.

Just look at his response to his needy siblings in Genesis 45: 4-7: "I am Joseph, your brother whom you sold into Egypt. But don't be angry with yourself that you did this to me, for God did it! He sent me here ahead of you to preserve our lives. These two years of famine will grow to seven, during which there will be neither plowing nor harvest. God has sent me here to keep you and our families alive so that you will become a great nation."

Think about the experiences of betrayal you have personally lived through. Is there any chance that you could consider responding as Joseph did? Is there any way you could stop thinking about the cause of your hurt and instead focus on the virtues of forgiving? Healing occurs when we allow love to penetrate our hearts and offer the sweet gift of mercy.

Chapter five explores the courage of David. His courage came from his great trust in his God. When Goliath the Philistine giant was threatening the Israeli army, young David shouted: "You come at me with a sword and a spear, but I come to you in the name of the Lord of the armies of heaven and Israel." (1 Samuel 17:45)

David's victory over Goliath with five smooth stones was the first of many illustrious acts of bravery. His youth was spent shepherding, fighting off bears and lions from his flock. His times in the fields gave him ample opportunity to sing praises and psalms to the greatness of the Lord.

He played his harp and sang for King Saul and then went on the run from the king for years after being anointed as the next king of Israel by the prophet Samuel. King Saul was merciless in chasing David, but David refused to touch a hair on the king's head even when he had the chance to avenge himself.

We find in examining David's life that he was a shepherd, a musician, a warrior, and a king. We see in him both the best and the worst of what humanity can be. For instance, when he saw beautiful Bathsheba bathing, he had her sent to his bedroom. When she became pregnant, he had her husband, Uriah, killed. His sins were horrible.

Yet through it all, David had an incredible bond with God. He is known as a man after God's own heart. David's life shows us what union with the Father means.

Have you, like David, done things you are ashamed of? In truth, we all have. But David's story gives us hope. If we will boldly trust in our mighty God, He will be with us and care for us. Like David, we can realize that the battle is not ours, but rather the Lord's.

God will not only give you a vision, He will also give you the passion, focus, and unwavering motivation to achieve that vision. But you must have the courage and hope to step out and find out.

In chapter six, we look at the strength of perseverance. Newt Gingrich once said that perseverance is the hard work you do after you get tired of doing the hard work you already did.

James 5:10 instructs us to take the old prophets as our mentors: "They put up with anything, went through everything, and never once quit, all the time honoring God. What a gift life is to those who stay the course!" (Message)

Do you have the wherewithal to put up with anything – to keep honoring God and stay the course? Perhaps the ancient story of Nehemiah will encourage you. It certainly encouraged me.

Nehemiah was a cupbearer for King Artaxerxes of Persia when he found out that the walls around Jerusalem were extensively broken-down. When he heard of the devastation, the first thing he did was sit down and weep. He cared – he cared a great deal. Do you have causes in life that you care deeply about? Do you have issues that bring you to tears? What are you willing to do about them?

Nehemiah began his careful response to the broken wall of Jerusalem by getting on his knees and fervently asking God for direction. Over and over again throughout Nehemiah's story, we see him slipping away into solitude to pray and seek God's will. Amazingly, Nehemiah spearheaded the rebuilding of the wall of Jerusalem in a mere fifty-two days.

If I could emulate one thing about Nehemiah it would be his habit of praying intensely for long periods of time before taking any action. I would like to have that kind of intimacy with my Maker.

At the right time, Nehemiah approached the city officials, saying, "You know full well the tragedy of our city; it lies in ruins and its gates are burned. Let us rebuild the wall of Jerusalem and rid ourselves of this disgrace." (Nehemiah 2:17)

After he diagnosed the problem, he took an active role in solving it. Nehemiah was successful in creating a team that could work together. Rebuilding the entire wall of Jerusalem was a daunting task. But Nehemiah prudently divided the work and assigned different parts of the plan to different groups. This helped make an overwhelming task more doable.

He also joined in on the work he organized. If you and I want to make the world a better place, we must get involved and do our part. We can encourage others with our own best efforts.

Once the wall was rebuilt, Nehemiah did the hardest possible thing for a leader – he handed authority over to Ezra because he was better qualified for creating the next steps in God's desires for Jerusalem.

Nehemiah went back to his job of cupbearer until he found out there were problems back in Jerusalem. He went back and corrected these issues with the beautiful servant's heart he had displayed throughout the entire process.

Nehemiah teaches us that we are not here merely to fulfill our own purposes. God created us to bring His purposes to fulfillment. I hope this book invites you to fulfill the purposes God created you for.

You can become a positive force in the world. You have a distinct and important purpose for living. You have specific strengths that God can use to further the work of His kingdom. As you look at the various stories of heroes in the Bible, it is my desire that you be able to apply the truths of their lives to your story. May you flourish in the beautiful unfolding of God's creative partnership with you. I believe it will be something very special.

2 FAITH: BELIEVING EVERY PROMISE FOR YOUR LIFE

"Does the God who lavishly provides you with his own presence, his Holy Spirit, working things in your life you could never do for yourselves, does he do these things because of your strenuous moral striving or because you trust him to do them in you? Don't these things happen among you just as they happened with Abraham? He believed God, and that act of belief was turned into a life that was right with God…So those now who live by faith are blessed along with Abraham, who lived by faith – this is no new doctrine! And that means that anyone who tries to live by his own effort, independently of God, is doomed to failure." (Galatians 3: 5-6, 9 Message)

Every single promise that God has made in His Word will be fulfilled. Reading and believing the Bible can clue you in as to what you can claim as your own from the Lord. In *Sparkling Gems from the Greek*, Rick Renner instructed, "If you're planning to take a long adventurous exciting faith journey, you better dive into the Word of God."[1]

When we know the Word, we know God's heart. We must, therefore, value an intimate communion with Him above all else. Out of that vibrant relationship, we get to know His will and can express desires that honor Him. It is imperative to place our faith solely in God to meet those desires and trust Him to lead us to the right desires. It is folly to try to live independently of God.

Paul explained in Galatians that God lavishes the Holy Spirit upon us. This is truly the greatest gift anyone could ever receive. If we have the Holy Spirit alive and active within us, our lives will assume an optimal level of functioning that far outweighs the value of mere riches or human glory.

We can do nothing to earn this great blessing. All we must do is believe in our Lord Jesus Christ's absolute power and sovereignty. In other words, it is not a matter of willpower on our part but a full realization of the limitlessness of God's power.

We must rest in God arms; we must live by faith. When guilt and shame snare our consciousness, we must run into His open arms. In our own might, we can never right the wrongs we have done. We are all sinners. The Bible's most important message is amazingly simple: Christ died for our sins. He paid the ultimate price so that we could come freely before God as though we had never transgressed His commands.

This freedom comes only through the power of believing. We must make a conscious act of the will to surrender the past completely to God, and then be done with it. Throw it away. He covers the stench of our sin, not because of any works we do, but because of who He is. If we are fully repentant, we must only believe. "Faith is the substance of things hoped for, the evidence of things not seen." (Hebrews 11:1, NKJV)

With that kind of faith, we can return to right relationships – both with God and our entire Christian family. All we are required to do is trust God completely. When we do, our lives will be restored. Blessings will emanate throughout our lives. God will even give us back everything the devil has stolen from us. We must hold firmly to the promise in Joel 2:25 in which God says, "I will repay you for the years the locusts have eaten."

To continue your growth with the Almighty, feed regularly on God's Word. Learn to apply basic truths to your everyday life. In this way, you will live an orderly, pleasing life, and be whole and happy. After all, faith is the opposite of fear.

What role has faith played in your life? Are you thriving with a strong, unflappable trust in God?

Did you know that the Bible tells us 365 times to "fear not?" That is one "fear not" for every day of the year. When we fear, we are demonstrating a lack of belief in God and what He can do for us. We need to break free and trust God completely. By believing every promise the Bible gives us, we can enjoy a dynamic life filled with purpose.

Abraham had just such a life. He always chose to "trust and obey" whenever and wherever God led him. Studying Abraham's life through the lens of positive psychology is affirming. Abraham awesomely depicted the character strength of faith. He trusted God so completely that he did not bother to worry about much of anything.

Abraham's story began in Genesis 11 and ended at chapter 25. In those fourteen chapters, Abraham stepped forward as a wonderful example of what can happen when a person chooses to have absolute faith in God regardless of the situation.

Genesis 12 reports Abraham's first major act of faith. God instructed him to leave the familiar friends and surroundings of his own country and depart for an undisclosed land.

Try to put yourself in his position. Surely it was extremely frightening and daring to leave behind everything familiar.

How do you think you would respond if God asked such a seeming gamble of you? There exists deep within you that same intensity of faith that God found in Abraham. That faith is there because, through Jesus, we Christians became the spiritual descendants of Abraham. I am sure Abraham felt great trepidation in leaving all he knew. Yes, he struck out for an unknown location, but what a grand adventure God took him on. He waits to do the same for you.

Because Abraham faithfully obeyed, God promised, "I will cause you to become the father of great nations; I will bless you and make your name famous, and you will be a blessing to many others. I will bless those who bless you and curse those who curse you; and the entire world will be blessed because of you." (Genesis 12: 2-3)

Throughout the unfolding of this story of beautiful intimacy between God and Abraham, God promised that Abraham's descendants would obtain the promised land of Canaan. He promised they would flourish there, and He compared Abraham's descendants to the countless stars in the big night sky.

Abraham's name had originally been Abram, but God changed it because Abraham means "father of nations." God made a covenant with Abraham that their relationship would continue from generation to generation and never end.

Abraham never doubted God's promises. He paused frequently to build altars in order to worship the Lord. Can you conceive of adopting this type of trusting attitude with God when you are facing enormous challenges? Do you see how faith grows a person's character? Can you sense how this trusting attitude brought success into Abraham's life? You can legitimately claim such an attitude for yourself as a spiritual descendant of Father Abraham.

In an excerpted article from his book *Become a Better You*, Joel Osteen said, "If you will have the right attitude, you will give birth to more in the future than you've lost in the past. Quit looking back. This is a new day. It may seem like your dreams have died, but God can resurrect your dead dreams and give you brand-new ones. He is a supernatural God, and when we believe, all things are possible."[2]

Perhaps you have a difficult past that makes it hard for you to relate to Abraham's great faith and obedience. If so, what Joel Osteen said becomes vitally important for your life. Letting go of the past and its mistakes is letting go of fear and trusting that with God in charge, your future will be a good one. If you can grasp that kind of faith, you can expect complete restoration. In order to reach that plane, however, you will have to trust God implicitly.

It could have been difficult for Abraham to believe he would have any descendants. He and his wife, Sarah, were very old, and she had been barren for many, many years. However, Abraham stood firm and believed God's Word. As promised, in their old age, the couple conceived and bore Isaac. Isaac's name meant "laughter" because Sarah laughed when the Lord predicted Isaac's birth. Eventually, God transferred the contract he had made with Abraham to Isaac and to all the posterity to come.

It is evident in reading Abraham's life story that he was not afraid to talk things over with God and make requests of Him. In Genesis 18, Abraham was so confident in his relationship with the Creator that he talked God into letting him try to find some godly folks in Sodom. God was angry because of the putrid sin abounding in the town and wanted to destroy everyone in it. Abraham bargained God down from finding fifty good men in Sodom to just ten. God promised to save Sodom if Abraham could find just ten good men in the adulterous city.

Because of Abraham's intercession on behalf of Sodom, his relative Lot and Lot's daughters were able to evacuate the area before God, in His disgust, destroyed it. Would you demonstrate the kind of faith and confidence

Abraham displayed in bargaining with God? Could you intercede and beseech the Lord to give wicked people just a little more time to turn their eyes and hearts over to Jesus? Is that not why God is waiting to return – so that as many people as possible can be saved from destruction?

We find Abraham's most amazing demonstration of absolute trust in and obedience to God in Genesis 22. God asked Abraham to do the unthinkable – to sacrifice the apple of his eye, his long-awaited, precious son, Isaac.

Surely Abraham's heart was breaking at the thought of slaying the much-cherished son through whom he was to propagate his descendants. Abraham, however, refused to question God. Nor did he argue.

Abraham could have exclaimed: "God, You can't be serious! You told me my descendants would be as dust, that I would not even be able to count their number. How can I ever have these promised descendants if You take my treasure, my heart, my special son?"

Nevertheless, Abraham did not question God at the moment of the most devastating possibility in his life. No. Stalwartly, Abraham walked up a hill with Isaac and prepared to offer Isaac as his ultimate sacrifice. What kind of depth of belief in God did Abraham have to be able to do as God instructed? Does it make you rethink your answers and priorities when God makes a difficult request of you?

Abraham lifted his hand to slay Isaac. At the last moment he was instructed, "Lay down the knife; don't hurt the lad in any way for I know that God is first in your life – you have not withheld even your beloved son from me." (Genesis 22:12)

Abraham demonstrated his faith by allowing nothing and no one to reign supreme over his love other than God Himself. We can only marvel at the depth of a love like that.

Contemplate the fact that although God saved Abraham from sacrificing Isaac, the day would come when God would require such a heart-wrenching agony of Himself. God loved us so much that He offered His beloved, only Son, Jesus, on the cross to save our souls.

Jesus came from Abraham's lineage. Through His shed blood we have become Abraham's spiritual descendants. Jesus lovingly gave you the ultimate gift of eternal life through the cross. He bore the punishment for every moral and spiritual wrong you have committed or will commit. He paid the price so He could declare you "not guilty." He loved you that much.

Let go of the condemning thought that you will never be good enough. It would be true if you were standing before God on your own, but you are not on your own. You are good enough because the blood Jesus sacrificially shed covers you. Jesus paid the price for your brand new life in Him. Now you are free to walk honorably in society.

While we know Jesus is God and that His thoughts are higher than ours, we can compare our lives to that of a human being: Abraham. Does Abraham's obedience intimidate you when you think about exercising your own faith? Lest we get too discouraged, let's look at some of his foibles.

Because his wife, Sarah, was so beautiful, Abraham would at times try to pass her off as his sister. He did this because he was afraid he would be killed by an amorous suitor who might want him out of the way. This deception greatly aggravated both the Pharaoh of Egypt and the ruler, Abimelech. They both tried to sleep with Sarah, not realizing she was Abraham's wife. God intervened so that both men returned Sarah safely to her husband. Doesn't it seem strange that Abraham had such faith in big issues but feared these men? How typically human he was.

A sadder infraction occurred when Sarah and Abraham grew impatient because they had not produced an heir. After all, they were growing extremely old, and still no sign of a child was forthcoming. So Sarah got a bright idea.

Have you ever had a bright idea? Have you ever figured out the "perfect" shortcut to make sure God's promises come to pass, only to realize that waiting on the Lord is a crucial part of His plan for your life?

Sarah's bright idea was this: since she had not conceived, she would give Abraham her handmaiden, Hagar. Through this channel, an heir could come forth. Abraham was as gullible to his wife's suggestion as Adam had been when Eve offered him the apple in the Garden of Eden. So Abraham took Hagar to bed, and she conceived Ishmael.

This was not a plan built on great insight or even common sense. Inevitably, Sarah grew exceedingly jealous and eventually insisted that Abraham banish Hagar and Ismael from their home.

The subsequent treatment Hagar and her son received was cruel and unjust. Have you ever found yourself in the ironic circumstance of blaming others for messing up the plan, when you yourself launched everything in the wrong direction?

Take heart! God never stopped loving Abraham and Sarah. His commitment to them never wavered. His promises never faltered. It was so because God's promises did not depend on Abraham and Sarah's obedience but on God's grace and faithfulness. All they had to do was accept the promises by faith. What was good for Sarah and Abraham is good for us today.

God took Abraham on an extended and fascinating journey. A similar opportunity is available to you today. Are you ready for an adventure with God?

If so, you must believe that every promise for your life can come true. What are these promises? The only way to discover them all is to read His divinely inspired Word, the Bible. Contained within the covers of God's Book are the answers to any questions you might have.

By all means, read the Bible. Start memorizing Scripture. Fill your mind with Words of life. Why not start by studying the Bible five minutes a day, and then incrementally add more to your devotional time'? Keep a list nearby of people who need your prayers. It is good to start small and not become legalistic in our time with God. We do not spend time in His Word to fulfill some requirement, we do it because we love the Word and want to improve the quality of our lives.

We can come to Him "as is" because He loves us even in our sinfulness. We love Him because He first loved us. We can trust that He has a good plan and purpose for our lives. All we have to do is cooperate with His Holy Spirit which dwells within us.

It is essential to wait on God's timing in our lives. However, a poor performance on our part will not thwart God's plan. He is compassionate and all powerful. There is no mess we can make that He will not clean up if we turn to Him for help.

We must have the strength and courage, even in our imperfect condition, to keep pursuing His will. God has wonderful things in store for us just as He did for Abraham. We just have to stand fast and have faith in Him who loves us completely.

It is not too late for you or for me. There is still time for God's design for our lives to come true. Yield all you have and all you are to Him. He can take plan B and make it better than plan A would have ever been. Get a vision for who you can be.

You are clay in the Potter's hands. Be moldable. Be pliant. But most of all, put all your belief in the Potter. There are no limits to what He can do in your life.

Mark 9: 20-24 depicts a desperate father pleading for Jesus to remove a terrible demon from his son. The child was writhing and foaming at the mouth. When Jesus asked how long the child had been suffering, the father replied, "Since he was very small, and the demon often makes him fall into the fire or into water to kill him. Oh, have mercy on us and do something if you can."

"If I can?" Jesus asked. "Anything is possible if you have faith." The father instantly replied, "I do have faith; oh, help me to have more."

No matter how desperate a situation you are in, regardless of the challenges you face, there is always the possibility of a miracle from God. Never give up. When your faith is wavering, be like the father in the Mark Chapter 9 story. Ask Jesus for help to believe. Then your faith, a living force within you, will continue to grow.

Positive psychologists are beginning to take notice of the beneficial effects spirituality can have on a person's life. Through scientific study, a connection between religious belief and well-being is evident. In an empirical body of literature, psychologists observed how religion and spirituality aid mental functioning, addiction problems, marital success, effective parenting, stress management, and coping with the death of a loved one.[3]

These psychologists look at faith under a basic concept called *transcendence*. People who have strengths in this area are able to forge connections to the larger universe and can find meaning in life. Under the umbrella of transcendence are awe, gratitude, playfulness, and spirituality.[4]

This research views spirituality as having coherent beliefs about the universe's higher purpose and meaning. It includes knowing where you fit within the larger scheme. It is having beliefs about the meaning of life that shape conduct and provide comfort.[5]

In the U.S., spirituality resonates primarily through the Judeo-Christian tradition. Ninety-five percent of Americans believe there is a God. Eighty-six percent believe God can be reached through prayer. Eighty-six percent identify religion as important or very important to them.[6]

Religion is fundamentally a search for the sacred. Once discovered, efforts must be made to hold on to what has been found. The sacred has to do with all that is holy, the concept of God the Divine, and transcendence. Sacred things are set apart from the ordinary and are worthy of respect and vereration.[7]

Believers consider a variety of things as sacred. Think of the Jewish Holy of Holies which only special priests could enter. Ponder the importance that believers associate with the Lord's Day. Contemplate the reverence given to buildings such as churches and temples. Big transitions such as birth and death have a sacred significance. Material items such as the bread and the wine or a crucifix have special meaning to believers. Sacred music and literature help people to experience their beliefs more fully.[8]

Leaders and fellow believers can deepen and add meaning to the spiritual journey. Community is highly valued. The sacred has to do with social attributes such as treating others with compassion.[9] As William Bennett stated in *The Book of Virtues*, "A shared faith binds people together in ways that cannot be duplicated by other means."[10]

The National Opinion Research Center has surveyed more than forty thousand Americans over three decades. The data indicate that people active in faith communities more often report being "very happy."[11]

This happiness occurs because these peoples' faith helps them understand the purpose of their existence. Meaning is derived from believing in Someone greater than oneself. That Someone, God, can give worth to the believer in a way nothing and no one else can. Holding a view of the sacred affects the way people conduct themselves in their marital, parental, and working lives.[12]

When we have goals concerned with ultimate purpose, ethics, and a commitment to God, we are striving to grow spiritually. Spiritual strivings are more highly related with measures of well-being than any other type of striving.[13] This means that even though our primary purpose in worship is to honor God, such worship also pays off in terms of greater psychological and physical health.

Prayer is another important aspect of interacting with the sacred. Some people feel comfortable with rituals, such as reading from a prayer book. Other people use prayers to make petitions for what they need. Often, prayer is a conversation. A believer might, for instance, talk to God and ask Him for forgiveness.[14]

Meditative prayer seems to be especially effective. A person meditates by choosing to just bask in God's presence. Spending time with the Lord and Creator deepens the relationship. Getting closer to God is a wonderful benefit. Of all types of prayer, this meditative posture is the most beneficial to overall health.[15]

Having a close relationship with God is especially helpful when someone is faced with difficult circumstances. With the Father's assistance, believers can maintain their faith in a just and loving God in the midst of trauma and loss. They can see a larger spiritual purpose behind a negative event. This is called *reframing*. It can help turn a crisis into a spiritually meaningful experience and an opportunity for growth.[16]

Much of psychology in America has been control focused. Making the unconscious conscious, increasing behavioral and cognitive control, and empowerment of the disempowered are all hallmarks of a psychological movement to help people develop greater control over their lives. The difficulty with all of this is, however, that some aspects of our lives are completely out of our control.[17]

Limits are a central part of the human condition. A spirituality that helps us come to terms with what is out of our control may conversely help improve a psychology attempting to enhance our power and control. The language of religion includes letting go, forbearance, suffering, faith, mystery, finitude, sacrifice, grace, and transformation.[18]

Seeking the sacred is a life-long pursuit. It begins in childhood. Young ones often have an amazing grasp on the Infinite. These are the words of a nine-year-old Jewish boy: "I'd like to find God! But He wouldn't just be there, waiting for some spaceship to land! He's not a person, you know! He's a spirit. He's like the fog and the mist. Maybe He's like something – something we've never seen here. So how can we know? You can't imagine Him, because He's so different – you've never seen anything like Him…I should remember that God is God, and we're us. I guess I'm trying to get from me, from us, to Him with my ideas when I'm looking up at the sky!"[19]

Artists and writers often seem to retain a child-like connection to the Divinity. These are the sentiments of Emily Dickenson in a poem entitled, *I Never Saw a Moor*:

I never saw a moor,

I never saw the sea;

Yet I know how the heather looks,

And what a wave must be.

I never spoke with God,

Nor visited in heaven;

Yet certain am I of the spot

As if the chart were given.[20]

Having faith in God is what makes life worth living. God wants to provide for you. You can believe that. Trust Him to meet all your needs. He longs to hold you close as a mother cradles her infant.

Kenneth Pargament and Annette Mahoney said it well: "Spirituality is a process that speaks to the greatest of our potentials. The capacity to envision, seek, connect, hold on to, and transform the sacred may be what makes us uniquely human."[21]

3 OPTIMISM: YES, WE CAN!

"Be strong and courageous, for you will lead my people to possess all the land I swore to give their ancestors. Be strong and very courageous. Obey all the laws Moses gave you. Do not turn away from them, and you will be successful in everything you do. Study this Book of the Law continually. Meditate on it day and night so you may be sure to obey all that is written in it. Only then will you succeed. I command you – be strong and courageous! Do not be afraid or discouraged. For the Lord your God is with you wherever you go." (Joshua 1: 6-9)

Life is full of opportunities to make decisions. You can see only the gloomy side of life or you can choose to look on the brighter side. You can despair or you can choose to keep a positive attitude in the midst of adversity. You can face your daily life with a sense of hopelessness or you can make a decision to cling to hope no matter what.

The crucial difference between a good decision and a bad decision is how you talk to yourself about it. A good decision occurs when you own your choice and have the courage to support that choice rather than continually doubting yourself and rehashing every move you make.

Joshua set a sterling example of resolute decision-making. Whenever God gave Joshua a command, no matter how unusual or difficult, he performed the task with optimism. The Lord appointed Joshua to usher the Israelites into the Promised Land. He did so with great pizzazz.

Joshua based his optimism on his relationship with an all-powerful, loving, and creative God. His confidence rested solely in the Lord and what He could do through His people.

Just like the Israelites in the Old Testament, you have the choice to turn your life completely over to God's will. When you give yourself to the Lord and cast your cares on Him, you can rest in the certainty that He will take care of you and help you live up to your full potential.

Joshua's mentor, Moses, trusted God completely. He was, however, timid and easily overwhelmed. Yet God saw Moses' humility and honored it.

Because he trusted God, Moses was the perfect leader to conduct the Israelites out of Egypt. Still, it was Joshua whom God equipped with the optimistic faith to usher them into the Promised Land.

When Joshua and Caleb looked over the Promised Land for the first time, they were positive that with God's help the Israelites could defeat the native tribes and inhabit the land successfully. Unfortunately, they were only two of twelve spies who completed a forty-day exploration of the Promised Land.

The other ten spies told the people that the situation was hopeless. Oh, it was true, they explained, that the land was "flowing with milk and honey." They had brought back luscious fruit as evidence of the Promised Land's abundance. However, the resident tribes were fierce, entrenched, and intimidating. They reported seeing Anakim giants so tall that the spies felt like grasshoppers before them. In their complete pessimism and fear, the ten spies rejected God's plan and sovereignty.

Caleb, however, reassured the people as they stood before Moses, "Let us go up at once and possess it, for we are well able to conquer it." (Numbers 13:30)

Caleb sided with Joshua, embracing the minority position. He agreed that Canaan was well fortified but he believed his God was mightier than any enemy. Yes, he saw the obstacles as clearly as the other spies. Despite the intimidation factor, he believed God's Word.

The Israelites chose to disregard Caleb and Joshua and accept the majority view. They refused to march into the land God had promised them. Caleb knew this was wrong and stood up for what was right. He was more interested in God's approval than the peoples'.

The situation may have appeared desperate, but Caleb knew that by turning his will and his life over to the Lord, he would achieve victory. Caleb had the optimism to grab on to the hope of all God had promised. He was reading the situation accurately and determining that his God was more powerful than any other existing force.

Perhaps there are portions of your life that seem hopeless. Just as it was for Caleb, so it is for you today. If you turn your will and life over to Jesus, your victory is incontrovertible. When trouble comes, that is the time to trust God the most.

Decide today that you will never give up until you have completed the race God has ordained for you to run. This decision will help you to grow in strength and resilience. Then when frustrations or failures bombard you, you will be able to quickly bounce back and achieve your victory.

When your heart is heavy with fear and disappointment after a setback, dispute the negative ruminations your mind might project. After a mistake, chalk it up to being human. Write down your automatic negative thoughts and then disagree with them. Trump your negative thinking by choosing to be more optimistic about your situation. Most importantly, fight back using God's Word as a tool.

You could quote, for example, Hebrews 10: 35, 38-39: "Do not throw away your confidence; it will be richly rewarded…My righteous one will live by faith. And if he shrinks back, my soul will have no pleasure in him. But we are not of those who shrink back and are destroyed, but of those who believed and are saved."

Affirm inside yourself that you choose to focus on the positive. Stir up the joy of the Lord. Relax, trusting that God's plan for your life is unfolding as it should because you have surrendered to Him completely. This is optimism.

Optimism is like an underground river running deep below the surface in the caverns of your innermost being. It is a choice that can become a way of life. When you choose optimism, your inner river runs strong, pure, and clear.

Choosing optimism is choosing calmness, balance, and increased physical health. It works as a buffer against depression. When you build the muscle of optimism, you can improve the quality of your life. It can help you achieve the joyful life that is your birthright as a Christian.

Optimism can encourage you to make positive changes in your life. It can inspire you to set some goals. It can prompt you to move forward on the cherished dreams you hold deep within your heart of hearts. With patience, creativity, and God's blessing, you can follow your bliss and achieve your mission.

God has desires for your life too. He wants you to feel respected and admired, as well as sought after and loved. Through His acceptance, embrace your personal power. If you are to live a fulfilling and authentic existence, you must take up the challenges God sends your way.

This was the choice both Joshua and Caleb made – and because of their faith, they were rewarded by being the only two of their generation to successfully enter the Promised Land. God greatly blessed them both.

God exclaimed, "But my servant Caleb is a different kind of man he has obeyed me fully. I will bring him into the land he entered as a spy, and his descendants shall have their fair share in it." (Numbers 14:24)

God strongly supported Joshua, too. When Moses was old and ready to die, God instructed him to hand the mantle of leadership over to Joshua. Moses was 120 years old when he presented Joshua to the people as their new commander. He reassured the Israelites that the Lord would deliver the Canaanites to them.

"Then Moses called for Joshua and said to him, as all Israel watched, 'Be strong! Be courageous! For you shall lead these people into the land promised by the Lord to their ancestors; see to it that they conquer it. Don't be afraid, for the Lord will go before you and will be with you, He will not fail nor forsake you.'" (Deuteronomy 31: 7-8)

The people of Israel were under a lot of what we today term *stress*. The old fight or flight syndrome was surely in full fury. In studying stress, researchers assert the importance of positive beliefs, such as optimism, in adapting to a negative situation.

Many patients with life-threatening illnesses say they learned they were stronger than they would have believed prior to their illness. Many began to see advantages in their situations of which they previously had been unaware, and they report they were able to appreciate and accentuate the positive aspects of their lives in a creative manner.[1] This is the wisdom gleaned from meeting tough life challenges head on.

In *A Psychology of Human Strengths*, Lisa Aspinwall and Ursula Staudinger stated, "That people deliberately accentuate the positive in life to better deal with the negatives is surely a human strength. That people can draw on these strengths without ignoring or diminishing the negative realities of their situations is also important."[2] This balanced viewpoint has been referred to as *flexible optimism*. This is not a rose-colored world, and reality must be acknowledged if you are to modulate a better way for yourself.

You put optimism into effect when you pursue a goal that is meaningful to you. You also need an expectancy that eventually you will be able to achieve that goal you set. To succeed, then, chose the positive attitude and aptitude of optimism in order to persist until you achieve that goal. In "Three Human Strengths," Charles Carver and Michael Scheier concluded, "…this translates…into building people's confidence about successful outcomes to the point where effort is self-sustaining. Put simply, the attempt is to turn pessimists into optimists."[3]

Dr. Richard Davidson from the University of Wisconsin-Madison confirmed that the adult brain is changeable or "plastic" as opposed to being completely set in adolescence. "What this means is that although an individual may be born with a predisposition toward gloominess or anxiety, the emotional floor plan can be altered, the brain's furniture moved to a more felicitous arrangement; with a little training, you can coax a fretful mind toward a happier outlook," he said.[4]

Aristotle's concept of *eudaimonic well-being* encapsulates a way of striving toward excellence based on one's unique talents and potential. Davidson commented, "The positive emotion accompanying thoughts that are directed toward meaningful goals is one of the most enduring components of well-being."[5]

Another way to increase happiness and optimism is to deliberately design your life around the activities that bring you the most joy. Small changes can make a big difference. For instance, take that afternoon walk around the lake. Spend time meditating. Bathe by candlelight.

Thinking about what you like and don't like, however, can also lead you to questioning some of your long-held assumptions.[6] If in your assessment you discover you are really hassled by your job and seldom enjoy it, you have some soul-searching and decision-making ahead.

Avoiding "if only" fantasies can rid your mind of a lot of negative thinking. Research indicates that most of us are surprisingly unaware of what will really make us happy.[7] If the "if only" had come to pass, the results might have been disastrous. You can be assured that if Christ is the Lord of your life, He will make your life a grander adventure than anything your limited mind could imagine.

Spending quality time with God is a great way to grow your optimism. Research has discovered, also, that spending quality time with a good friend can boost your level of positive emotion. The nature of the relationship is the crucial element in friendships. More joy arises from hanging out longer periods of time with a close chum.[8]

Some of us, deep down, feel it is wrong to be happy and upbeat when so many people are suffering. The truth is, happy people are in more of a position to help the needy than a die-hard pessimist would be.[9] Keeping yourself in a mirthful mood can contribute to peace on earth.

In *Lighten Up: Survival Skills for People under Pressure*, C.W. Medcalf and Roma Feliable explained, "Humor is a way of seeing, salving and solving the serious issues of our lives…Now it may be that what we need to do most is to learn to laugh a little more, to take ourselves – even our pain – a little less seriously."[10]

Red Skelton, the famous comedian, once said, "I live by this credo: Have a little laugh at life and look around you for happiness instead of sadness. Laughter has always brought me out of unhappy situations."[11]

In truth, optimism is a very serious business. Most of the developed world is "experiencing an unprecedented epidemic of depression – particularly among young people," said Martin Seligman in *Learned Optimism*. "Severe depression is ten times more prevalent today than it was fifty years ago. It assaults women twice as often as men, and it now strikes a full decade earlier in life on average than it did a generation ago."[12]

Learned helplessness is synonymous with depression. It is a state of believing that you are trapped, that you have no choices, and that there is no way to avoid failure. It is reacting to the challenges of your life by giving up and quitting. It makes a person feel that whatever he or she would do does not matter. This is a pessimistic explanatory style.

An optimistic explanatory style stops helplessness. The way you explain events to yourself determines how helpless you become. How are you at explaining everyday setbacks or momentous defeats to yourself? What you think and tell yourself will determine whether you grow more helpless or instead choose to believe you can change your lot and so become energized to do so.[13]

You can be encouraging to yourself when facing difficulties. This can dramatically change the outcome of your challenge. It can mean the difference between success and failure.

You can learn to increase your level of optimism and control over your life by thinking realistically and refusing to view adversity as a catastrophe.

"When bad events strike, you don't have to look at them in their most permanent, pervasive, and personal light, with the crippling results that the pessimistic explanatory style entails," Seligman said.[14] This means realizing the adversity is not permanent but rather temporary. One bad grade at school does not have to mean you will fail to graduate.

You can avoid a pervasive sense of helplessness by working to contain a difficulty to the particular life area in which you are struggling. Do not allow the situation to be disabling across the dimensions of your home, work, leisure, and social lives. When a loved one dies, for instance, getting back to work after appropriate grieving can help you feel more in control of your life.

It is also crucial to learn not to take things personally. Most of the time when people mistreat you, it is coming from something inside of them that they have not figured out how to master on the emotional level. Realizing this can save you many hours of anger, hostility and rumination.

It is very helpful to dispute your negative distortions. When you find yourself responding to a situation with helplessness and depression, argue with yourself. Keep up the pep talk until you feel better. Then think about what you can do to improve a situation.

By taking these steps, your health and general well-being will increase.

"Findings show that learned helplessness doesn't just affect behavior; it also reaches down to the cellular level and makes the immune system more passive," Seligman said.[15]

These findings are interesting in light of researcher Daniel Gilbert's comparison of the psychological immune system with the physical immune system. That is, the mind defends against unhappiness much the way the body defends against illness. The physical body strikes a balance between recognizing and destroying foreign invaders like viruses while respecting the body's own cells. Likewise the psychological immune system must not defend you too well ("I'm perfect and everyone is against me") and must not fail to defend you well enough ("I am a loser and I ought to be dead.") Stick to the facts and realize that rather than being defenseless or defensive, you need to be tenderly defended by your own self-talk.[16]

William James, the father of American psychology, wrote *The Varieties of Religious Experience*. It was a bold tribute to the view that religion "gives some serenity, moral poise, and happiness, and prevents certain forms of disease as well as science does, or even better."[17]

This thinking is right in line with that of Joshua and Caleb. Both were optimists and were able to flourish amid great adversity. It was Joshua's job to secure his people in the land God had given to them. There was a great weight of responsibility on his shoulders. Nevertheless, he was an optimist and a believer.

The Israelites fought many battles to win their beloved Promised Land. The most famous was the Battle of Jericho. You can find it in children's Bible storybooks and in Sunday school lessons for all ages.

God told Joshua, "Jericho and its king and all its mighty warriors are already defeated, for I have given them to you!" Of course, Joshua had complete faith in what the Lord told him.

The entire army walked around the city of Jericho once a day for six days, followed by seven priests walking ahead of the Ark, each carrying a trumpet. On the seventh day, they all walked around the city seven times with trumpets blowing. With one loud blast, the people shouted and the walls of the city fell down. Then the Israelite army moved in from all directions. (see Joshua 5:2)

Gibeon was the spot for another memorable battle. At Joshua's request, God allowed the sun and moon to stand still so that the Israeli army could complete the destruction of their enemies.

"So Joshua took the entire land just as the Lord had instructed Moses; and he gave it to the people of Israel as their inheritance, dividing the land among the tribes. So the land finally rested from its war." (Joshua 11:23)

Right before his death at 110 years old, Joshua admonished the people to "revere Jehovah and serve Him in sincerity and truth." (Joshua 24:14)

Yes, Joshua was faithful. He was a thriver as well. Perhaps as you face your challenges, whether family issues, job stress, or chronic illness, you can reflect on how Joshua and Caleb conducted themselves in difficult times. With optimism in your heart, you can say along with Joshua and Caleb, "Yes, we can!"

Optimism believes in the best. It is having the hope that good things will happen. It is letting go of yesterday after learning whatever lessons yesterday offered, and moving forward into a world of brand-new possibilities.

Dietrich Bonhoeffer, a Lutheran pastor and theologian who participated in the German Resistance movement against Nazism once said, "The essence of optimism is that it…enables a man to hold his head high, to claim the future for himself and not abandon it to his enemy."[18]

Life is not an ordeal to be survived; it is an adventure of choices to be lived. I hope you choose optimism and joy.

4 FORGIVENESS: LET GO AND BE FREE

"Then if my people will humble themselves and pray, and search for me, and turn from their wicked ways, I will hear them from heaven and forgive their sins and heal their land. I will listen, wide awake, to every prayer made in this place. For I have chosen this temple and sanctified it to be my home forever; my eyes and my heart shall always be here." (2 Chronicles 7: 14-16)

This verse contains one of God's most wonderful promises. He made it specifically to Israel, but it can be fulfilled in our lives today as well. Because Jesus went to the cross for us, God listens to our prayers. He will forgive our sins if we confess them. This truth can give us great comfort as we deal with failure, and it can help us extend mercy to those we need to forgive.

Forgiving and receiving forgiveness unfold together as a process requiring time and commitment. Stress infuses our fast-paced lives. We often find it difficult to slow down and attend to our spiritual and emotional needs. We rush around irritable and impatient, and seldom take the time to get to the heart of our problems.

Many of us are carrying around heavy burdens. Toxic emotions such as anger, disgust, and guilt block our effectiveness and level of fulfillment. Sometimes we direct these destructive emotions toward others, and sometimes we direct them toward ourselves. Fortunately, God has provided a healthy way to meet our hurts and needs through the power of forgiveness. He can show us how to let go and be free.

The first step toward getting right with God involves our taking an honest personal inventory. This step inevitably leads to the recognition of sin in our lives.

First John 1: 8-9 declared, "If we claim we have no sin, we are only fooling ourselves and not living in the truth. But if we confess our sins to him, he is faithful and just to forgive us from all wickedness." This cleansing from sin is possible through the blood Jesus shed for each of us.

We have needed God's forgiveness since Adam and Eve's fall in the

Garden of Eden. When Adam and Eve failed, God set His plan of redemption into play by sending the second Adam, His perfect Son, Jesus Christ, to die for our transgressions.

The Holy Spirit repeatedly warns us to stay away from sin. Like Adam and Eve, however, we sometimes stray from God's will. Thankfully, through Jesus, God has provided a way to reconnect. First John 2: 1-2 declared, "But if anyone does sin, we have an advocate who pleads our case before the Father. He is Jesus Christ, the one who is truly righteous. He himself is the sacrifice that atones for our sins – and not only our sins, but the sins of all the world."

Think of Jesus hanging on the cross. His concern was not for Himself but for others. He directed His compassion toward those who were torturing Him. He hung there in humiliation, more totally alone than we could ever understand; and in His darkest hour He prayed, "Father, forgive them, for they do not know what they do." (Luke 23: 34 NKJV)

Jesus Christ is the great resource and advocate for all of us. He received the full force of God's anger against sin so we do not have to experience God's anger for our past, present, and future sins. When we believe Christ suffered for our sins, we can come to the Father freely. We can approach Him with complete trust that He will accept us unconditionally. What a miracle! The God of the universe is willing to bind our wounds and care for us just as we really are.

Since we accept the great gift of God's forgiveness toward our sin, we need to give that same sort of forgiveness to those who have hurt us. Colossians 3:13 instructs, "Bearing with one another and forgiving one another, if anyone has a complaint against another; even as Christ forgave you, so you also must do." (NKJV)

Forgiveness is the act of excusing an offense and granting a pardon. It is letting go of resentment. If we hold on to resentment, it can drive us to despair or anger. It can cause us to play scenes over and over again in our minds until we nearly break apart with pain and hurt. Relief can seem hopelessly far away. Being unable to forgive keeps our emotions in an uproar, blocking the serenity and peace our minds crave. Is anything really worth that price?

The truth is that the past is gone and God wants us to look forward rather than back. In Isaiah 43: 18-19 the Lord said, "Do not remember the former things, nor consider the things of old. Behold, I will do a new thing, now it shall spring forth; shall you not know it? I will even make a road in the wilderness and rivers in the desert." (NKJV)

Paul expressed a similar sentiment in Romans 12:2: "Be not conformed to this word; but be ye transformed by the renewing of your mind, that ye may prove what is that good, and acceptable, and perfect will of God." (KJV)

What if we dumped our baggage and left it in a wasteland never to be found again? What if we developed a genuine attitude of forgiveness? What if we allowed our burdens to lift, leaving us free to love others and ourselves fully? We could work to eliminate guilt, resentment, embarrassment, sadness, and hurt, and to fill our minds with satisfaction and joy instead.

The most effective way to do this is to speak God's Word. If we say aloud what He says in the Bible, we find ourselves on a path to wonderful health.

Look up the topic of forgiveness in your Bible concordance. Write the verses that touch you on index cards so you can say and review them.

In his book *Authentic Happiness*, Martin Seligman spoke of rewriting your past.[1] The concept of rewriting history means you can remember the good parts of the past and reframe the not-so-good parts. Fully enjoy the good memories from the past and reframe the painful parts. Find a way to think about them without feeling pain or regret.

Sometimes it helps to simply accept what happened. It also helps to decide to forgive regardless of your feelings. The perspective of time helps us see formerly hurtful situations with more compassion. What a lift to be able to look back with eyes of love and forgiveness!

This process usually takes place in stages. As we practice forgiveness over time, we can eventually expect to feel our negative emotions slipping away. If the memories come flooding back occasionally, we can make a conscious effort to practice forgiveness again. Each time we choose forgiveness over judgment, we achieve a private victory.

Each time we choose compassion over a critical spirit, we take a step forward. No effort we make, no matter how small, is ever wasted. We must never give in to the mistaken belief that our efforts to become more forgiving are in vain. God notices every time we release a hurt from our past. He rejoices as He sees us let resentments go.

The longer we practice forgiveness the more our brains get into a healthy balance and a state of equilibrium. If we keep practicing, we can reach a peaceful internal place in which we can charitably forgive the foolish mistakes of the past.

At each point in the journey toward total forgiveness of others and yourself, take your emotional temperature to see how you are progressing. Do you wish you could make the other person pay or that something bad would happen to him or her? Do you avoid being around the person or have trouble treating him or her warmly? Do you want to see the person miserable or hurt? Do you have thoughts about severing the relationship?[2] Can you let go and move further along the continuum toward freedom and forgiveness?

If anyone in the Old Testament had a reason to feel vengeful, it was Joseph. Yet he never wallowed in self-pity. Joseph's story is found in Genesis, which records mankind's birth and early history. Joseph is considered one of the four great patriarchs of the faith. Abraham, Isaac, and Jacob, Joseph's father, preceded him.

Jacob favored Joseph over all his brothers and so gave him a beautiful coat of many colors to show his love. As a young man, Joseph had a vision and a dream for his life. His boasting about this did not set well with his brothers.

His brothers sold him into slavery. An Egyptian military leader, Potiphar, purchased Joseph as a slave and put him to work. Soon Joseph was running all of Potiphar's business affairs. When Potiphar's wife failed to seduce Joseph, she falsely accused him of assaulting her. He was then hauled off to jail.

Joseph had such leadership ability that he was soon helping run the jail. He also displayed a propensity to be able to interpret dreams. After several years of imprisonment, one of the king's court remembered how Joseph had accurately deciphered dreams. So, Joseph was called before the

Pharaoh.

People in the ancient Near East attached great significance to dreams. The Egyptians and the Babylonians compiled books of sample dreams with keys to their interpretation. Joseph's interpretations always lined up with that of the Egyptian dream literature. But his stellar ability to accurately explain dreams came from God.[3]

Pharaoh called for Joseph and told of his dream that seven fat cows were consumed by seven skinny ones. Then he dreamed that seven beautiful ears of corn were followed by seven tattered and torn ears. Joseph explained the dreams: There would be seven years of plenty followed by seven years of drought. If the country stored the excess, everyone would survive the famine.

In time, Pharaoh made Joseph his second-in-command. He put Joseph in charge of keeping resources available for Egypt and the surrounding lands to prepare for times of famine and drought.

In Genesis 42: 21-22 we learn that Joseph's brothers arrived in Egypt because they were running out of food. Eventually they realized that the highly positioned administrator they were asking for help was actually Joseph – the brother they had abused and sold into slavery so many years before.

Speaking among themselves, they murmured, "This has all happened because of what we did to Joseph long ago. We saw his terror and anguish and heard his pleadings, but we wouldn't listen."

Have you ever been in a position like that of Joseph's brothers? Isn't it terrible to realize that horrible sins have been committed for which you have no good excuse or defense?

Instead of punishing his brothers, however, Joseph freely forgave them. Perhaps he even chuckled to himself as he saw how God had brought them all full circle. He would not have been able to help anyone had he not been mistreated at strategic points in his life.

In Genesis 45: 4-7 he called the brothers to come closer, and said, "I am Joseph, your brother, whom you sold into slavery in Egypt. But don't be upset and don't be angry with yourselves for selling me to this place. It was God who sent me here ahead of you to preserve your lives. This famine that has ravaged the land for two years will last five more years, and there will be neither plowing nor harvesting. God has sent me ahead of you to keep you and your families alive and to preserve many survivors."

The writers of the *Archeological Study Bible* suggest, "Study the life of Joseph, from his years of slavery to his meteoric rise to power in a strange land to his revelation to his unsuspecting brothers. This book [Genesis] explains how and why the Israelites came to live in Egypt, setting the stage for what would happen to this special people in Exodus and beyond." [4]

In his magnanimity, Joseph foreshadowed the life and actions of Christ, who makes all things work together for good for those who love the Lord and are called according to his purpose. (see Romans 8:28)

When we forgive, marvelous things happen. When we forgive, we give people a second chance. When we forgive, our guiding principle becomes not revenge, but mercy.

In her ministry to countless people, Joyce Meyer shares the experience of years of sexual abuse she endured from her father.[5] Looking back, after much suffering and many years of reflection, she fully believes God's Word in Joel 2:25: "I will restore to you the years that the swarming locust has eaten." (NKJV)

Moreover, she believes she is more successful, has better character, and can help more people because of all she has been through. Instead of resisting what happened, Joyce accepts what happened. She even believes God can use her suffering ultimately to do more good than if she had never been so deeply wounded.[6]

Joyce explains that even if we had no other reason to forgive, we must do it because God said so. He expects His children to obey His dictates. Without forgiveness, our relationship to Him is blocked. She asks, "What is so unforgivable that I would let it hinder my personal relationship with God?"[7]

She points out that forgiveness is a choice. Despite extreme physical, emotional, and sexual abuse, Joyce has chosen to forgive. Look at all the success she has and all the help she has been able to give others because of that choice!

Joyce emphasizes that this is a process. Even after a person chooses to forgive, it will take time for his or her feelings to catch up with that decision. We must not lose faith just because our feelings at times disagree with the decision we have made to forgive. Studying the Word can help us discern how to handle our emotions properly. After forgiving, we can stand firm in the fact that we have done our part and now God will do His part.[8]

It is not easy, but it is the right thing to do. Forgiveness gives a peace and freedom that nothing else can. Jesus said, "I say to you who are listening now to Me: [in order to heed, make it a practice to] love your enemies, treat well (do good to, act nobly toward) those who detest you and pursue you with hatred, invoke blessing upon and pray for the happiness of those who curse you, implore God's blessing (favor) upon those who abuse you [who revile, reproach, disparage, and high-handedly misuse you.]" (Luke 6: 27-28 AMP)

What we are actually doing in this process of forgiving is asking God to bless the person with His presence. The truth is that most of the time people have no idea of the hurt they have inflicted upon us. When we bless someone, we speak well of him or her. We can say, with Jesus, "Father, forgive them, for they know not what they do." (see Luke 23:34)

Love covers a multitude of sins. This means that in love you can reach the point where you make excuses for your enemies. You can cover the one who hurt you by saying that the person did not understand what he or she was doing.

When you obey the Word of the Lord, Luke 6:35 stated, "your recompense (your reward) will be great (rich, strong intense, and abundant), and you will be sons of the Most High." (AMP)

Joyce explained, "We will get double for our trouble if we will do things His way."[9] I'd like that kind of reward. Wouldn't you?

In *Conflict-free Living*, Joyce wrote a chapter entitled, "Make Forgiveness a Lifestyle." She opened with, "I lived far too long behind walls I had built to protect myself from emotional pain because I was determined not to give anyone a chance to hurt me a second time…I was no longer being abused, but I held the abuse in my heart. It continued to cause pain in my life because I refused to trust God to vindicate me."[10]

Can you relate to what Joyce shared? Life's hurts can cause us to harden our hearts as a protection from more pain. But the answer lies not in shielding our hearts through unforgiveness, but rather in giving our hearts fully and completely into God's care. He will never fail to take care of us when we trust in Him.

The truth is when we refuse to forgive others, we open a door for the devil to torment us. The devil is always trying to stir up hatred and bitterness. He loves to see us feel disappointed with the circumstances of our lives, because that can develop into a disappointment with God Himself. Forgiveness and trust in God safely close the doorway to our hearts so that the devil cannot build a stronghold of anger and strife there.

Peter asked Jesus how many times he should forgive someone. He wondered if seven times would be sufficient. Jesus answered, "I tell you, not up to seven times, but seventy times seven." (see Matthew 18: 21-22)

Being longsuffering develops character. Having character gives us a strong foundation on which to build successful lives. Joyce concluded by encouraging each of us to "make forgiveness a lifestyle by choosing to trust Him with the things you don't understand."[11]

We will not have all the answers until we meet Jesus face to face. While in this world we see through a glass darkly. Even though we don't understand now, we will then. And if we are obedient to God's Word, we will build up a storehouse of treasures in heaven by following the examples of Joseph and Jesus.

Forgiveness is such an important component of your walk with Jesus. When you forgive others by trusting in Him, Jesus takes you to higher and deeper levels of relationship with Him. So be gentle and forbearing when people lack insight or discretion.

Positive psychology has demonstrated that revenge has corrosive effects. Retaliation leads to escalating cycles of vengeance and is implicated in much of the violence that plagues our world.[12]

When someone is behaving badly, we can refuse to respond negatively. There is a lot of strength in that.

What is this character strength we call "forgiveness?" It is "a freely chosen motivational transformation in which the desire to seek revenge and to avoid contact with the transgressor is lessened, a process sometimes described as an altruistic gift," said Frank Fincham and Todd Kashdan in *Positive Psychology in Practice*.[13]

Don't confuse forgiveness with similar constructs. It is not the act of living in a state of denial, refusing to acknowledge your injury. Also, it is not the act of condoning the other person's actions. The offense happened. The hurt was real. Forgiveness is not the act of giving a pardon as a judge would. It is not synonymous with forgetting, nor does it necessarily involve reconciliation.

Forgiveness is a decision, and a wise one at that. There is now MRI evidence to show that forgiveness activates a specific region of the brain. The activation in the brain is so precise that it can be distinguished from empathy.[1]

Decreased hostility enhances physical health. Forgiveness fights heart disease and lessens hormonal and physiological responses to stress. But to be effective, forgiveness must come out of a heart of love rather than from an insincere gesture made out of a sense of obligation.[15]

The link between forgiveness and mental health shows that people who have been "helped to forgive someone" are more successful in overcoming addictions, guilt, and discouragement. Any improvement in relationships with others boosts mental health.

Being preoccupied with blame or ruminating on an injustice can be seen as a refusal to forgive. This is unhealthy mentally and physically.[16]

The amount of time a person spends thinking about forgiveness is critical to his or her success in forgiving. Thinking about the hurt without pondering the virtues of forgiving the cause of that hurt is counterproductive.[17]

Research has demonstrated that training childhood sexual abuse victims in how to forgive properly increases hope and self-esteem while decreasing anxiety and depression. The changes were maintained over a yearlong period.[18]

Interventions that can help with forgiveness include writing about past traumatic experiences. Enhancing relationship abilities like basic communication skills has been shown to be helpful as well.[19]

Some of these techniques have been implemented successfully with reformed criminals, said Finchman and Kashdan: "By allowing for forgiveness, restorative justice programs empower the victim and allow the perpetrator to be affirmed both by the victim and the community as a person of worth and to regain – or for many gain for the first time – their respect and be reintegrated – or integrated – into society."[20]

We are all sinners in search of redemption. Healing occurs in a context where we are prepared to let love penetrate our hearts to give and receive forgiveness out of a place of warmth, affection, and tenderness.

Do you want everything God can do for you? Do you wish to reach your full potential? The only way to achieve these outcomes is through obedience. If you will humble yourself and pray, both to forgive and be forgiven, your level of personal fulfilment will deepen. God asks you to turn from your evil ways. Those evil ways include nursing grudges. Think of the pleasure you will give God if you make your search to know Him better worth anything – even if it means forgiving a horrendous offense.

Copy Jesus' example by practicing forgiveness until it becomes a basic trait of your character. Think of all the possibilities that can manifest by releasing old hurts.

5 COURAGE: I COME TO YOU IN THE NAME OF THE LORD

"David shouted in reply, 'You come to me with a sword and a spear, but I come to you in the name of the Lord of the armies of heaven and of Israel – the very God whom you have defied. Today the Lord will conquer you, and I will kill you and cut off you head; and then I will give the dead bodies of your men to the birds and wild animals, and the whole world will know that there is a God in Israel! And Israel will learn that the Lord does not depend on weapons to fulfill his plans – he works without regard to human means! He will give you to us.'"(1 Samuel 17:45-47)

Like the cowardly lion in *The Wizard of Oz*, we all want to possess courage. With threats of terrorism, natural disasters, and random crime, there seems to be plenty to frighten us. But we also have fears about ourselves. We wonder if we have the strength to be the best people we can be – the people God created us to be. We fear we will fail to complete the mission God has planned for us.

We can find an answer to our deepest fears and anxieties through a personal, dynamic relationship with Jesus Christ. When we turn our lives over to Him, we receive all His blessings and protection. Psalm 31:24 challenges: "Be strong and let your heart take courage all you who wait for and hope for and expect the Lord!" (AMP)

Often we think of courage as a facing of fears through the sheer force of willpower. This is not a correct understanding of courage. Ultimately, courage is not something we muster out of our own power. Trusting the Lord opens a gateway through which courage can flow. It requires holding fast to hope and waiting patiently with faith for God to act. To be truly courageous we must believe in and expect that the omnipotent God will do what is best. We must believe he will act in His time, which is always the right time. And we must stand our ground until He does.

Think of the courage young David displayed as he faced the giant Goliath. He boldly stepped forward to recover the dignity of his people, the

Israelites. He shouted to Goliath, "You come at me with a sword and a spear, but I come to you in the name of the Lord of the armies of heaven and Israel." (1 Samuel 17:45)

William Bennett in *The Book of Virtues*, quotes Aristotle from his *Nicomachean Ethics*: "We become brave by doing brave acts…by being habituated to despise things that are terrible and to stand our ground against them we become brave, and it is when we have become so that we shall be most able to stand our ground against them."[1]

David's days as a protective shepherd – fighting off bears and lions – stood him in good stead to face Goliath. As we examine David's life, we see him as a shepherd, a musician, a warrior, and a king. Also, in him, we see the best and worst characteristics of humanity.

Throughout his life, David had an incredible bond with God. He was called a man after God's own heart. We would be wise to emulate the kind of intimate relationship David had with God. For each of us, nothing is more important than a vital union with our Savior. David's story gives us a blueprint as to what that union can look like.

In some symbolic ways, David prefigured Jesus Christ. In fact, the two shared a common genealogy. Both were descendants of Judah, one of the sons of Jacob. Through our study of David, we gain insights into the meaning of Christ's life. Although David's life was far from perfect, it foreshadowed details of Christ's story.

Let's delve into 1 and 2 Samuel, portions of 1 and 2 Chronicles, as well as some of the Psalms to discover who David was and what he was all about. We encounter David for the first time in 1 Samuel 16. God spoke to Samuel the prophet, telling him Saul was no longer fit to be the king of Israel. He then sent Samuel to Jesse of Bethlehem. One of Jesse's sons, the Lord said, was to be the next king.

Samuel studied each of Jesse's sons but none of them seemed right. Samuel asked Jesse if he had any more sons. Jesse explained that his youngest, David, was off tending sheep. Samuel insisted that Jesse summon David at once.

Just as Samuel found David, we can trust that no matter where we are or what we are doing, when God needs us to fulfill His purposes, He will find us. We will be right where we are supposed to be, learning exactly what we need to learn to fulfill our destiny.

In David's case, shepherding taught him a great deal. Psalm 78: 70-72 tells us, "He chose David his servant and took him from the sheep pens; from tending the sheep he brought him to be the shepherd of his people Jacob, of Israel his inheritance. And David shepherded them with integrity of heart; with skillful hands he led them." (NIV)

God had been preparing David all his life. He has also been preparing you. The challenges you deal with are much like the bear and lion David slew while tending his flock – preparation. David's adventures led him from the grazing field to the battlefield.

David's first job in the palace was playing the harp for King Saul, but eventually he became the king over all of Israel. Be open to the places God may be taking you.

As Beth Moore put it in *A Heart Like His*, "Never assume to follow Him means to throw away who He has made you to be. Few things seem less spiritual than keeping a bunch of smelly sheep, yet God used David's skills for eternal purposes."[2]

Think about your experiences, your strengths, and your talents. Realize that God made you with the same potential that David possessed. You were created for a unique and important purpose. How might the aptitude of courage help you grow into the Christian you want to be? How might such an attitude lead you to the same overwhelming success David experienced?

First Samuel 16:13 explained, "So Samuel took the horn of oil and anointed him in the presence of his brothers, and from that day on the Spirit of the Lord came upon David in power." (NIV) You can receive that same power if you will only invite the Holy Spirit into every area of your life.

Samuel finished his duty faithfully as the last of Israel's judges. The Israelites wanted a king to call their own, as the other nations had. At their insistence, Saul became the first king of Israel. He reigned for forty-two years.

Saul was self-centered, selfish, and insecure. As a leader, he was afraid of people, and so he became a people pleaser. This was a big mistake. We must always rank pleasing God, not others, as life's highest priority.

David knew this truth even as a young man. If he feared God, he would not have to fear man. He was taking his older brothers some supplies when he heard Goliath, the nine-foot-tall warrior, taunting the Israelites as he had done morning and night for forty days.

David was incensed. "Who is this uncircumcised Philistine that he should defy the armies of the living God?" he asked. (1 Samuel 17:26 NIV) He volunteered to fight the menacing giant.

Saul tried to give his personal armor to David. It did not fit. It was uncomfortable. David rejected the armor and chose instead to be comfortable in his own skin as he battled Goliath.

Are you comfortable in your skin as you fight your battles? Are you so intimate with God that you know He sees you as the victor before the fight even begins? Do you approach every circumstance with the confidence that befits a member of God's army? Do you have the faith that God is active and alive – that He loves you and wants to bless you through every obstacle you encounter?

David trusted God completely. He met Goliath with five smooth stones and a shepherd's slingshot. No giant will ever be as big as God is. No weapons will be too small to defeat the enemy if those weapons come from God. Even stones and a slingshot will do. David knew this, and because of his faith, he was victorious.

David was extremely brave. The *Values in Action Classification of Character Strengths Inventory* describes bravery as an aspect of courage. Bravery means refusing to shrink from a challenge or difficulty. It is acting upon one's convictions even if they are unpopular.[3] David was brave in facing Goliath because he trusted his God to be with him.

There was perhaps only one facet of David's life that might have made him prouder than defeating Goliath. That was his lifelong devoted friendship and covenant with Jonathan.[4] Look at what happened right after Goliath's defeat.

After King Saul had finished a conversation with David, David met Jonathan, the king's son. There was an immediate bond of love between them. Jonathan swore to be David's blood brother "and he sealed the pact by giving him his robe, sword, bow, and belt." (1 Samuel 18:4)

Somehow, Jonathan knew David was destined to be Israel's next king. Although he was the heir apparent for the job, Jonathan believed the crown should rest on David's head. He did all he could to protect David, even at grave risk to himself.

Years after Jonathan had died, David remembered Jonathan's son, Mephibosheth, who was crippled early in life. When David found him, he brought him into the palace to eat daily at the king's table. (see 2 Samuel 9:7)

David never forgot the unconditional love Jonathan had shown him. In doing so, David exhibited another characteristic that the *Values in Action Classification of Character Strengths* lists as a subset of courageousness – David acted authentically. He genuinely and without pretense wanted to show his willingness to take responsibility for Mephibosheth out of the love he cherished for Jonathan.[5] Perhaps the deep grieving David experienced when Jonathan died was softened by giving Mephibosheth a comfortable life.

King Saul had no such sentiments toward David. After Goliath's defeat, David became commander of Israel's troops. As the victorious Israeli army returned home from a battle with the Philistines, everyone was singing and dancing with tambourines and cymbals. They exulted: "Saul has slain his thousands, and David his ten thousands!" (1 Samuel 18:7)

This celebration greatly angered Saul, and he kept a jealous watch on David from that time on.[6] Ironically, the only thing that soothed Saul's tormented spirit was David's harp playing. One day as David was playing music for Saul, Saul hurled a spear at David. David quickly moved out of its path. This scenario was soon repeated, but David jumped out of the way again.

Saul banned David from his presence and demoted him, but David continued to succeed in everything he did. Scripture reports that God left Saul and went with David. This divine act frightened Saul, as did David's popularity with the people. According to 1 Samuel 18:16, "All Israel and Judah loved [David] for he was one of them."

David always proceeded with zest. The *Values in Action Classification of Character Strengths* describes *zest* as approaching life with excitement and energy, living life as an adventure, and feeling alive and activated.[7]

Unfortunately, Saul wasn't feeling very zestful. It was becoming obvious that Saul wanted David dead. He used any and all tactics to snare David. Saul's daughter, Michal, was in love with David. So Saul sent her to be married to David even though the young man had no dowry.

Saul set the price for the bride at "a hundred Philistine foreskins." (1 Samuel 18:25) Saul planned for David to die in battle. Michal double-crossed her father and helped David escape when Saul pursued him.[8] Jonathan did the same.[9]

Saul is a study in failed leadership. The culture of a company, or in this case, a kingdom, is determined by the way a leader communicates attitudes and standards. People are strongly influenced by a leader's behavior. To direct successfully, the leader must be willing to tolerate and even encourage open confrontation and debate as well as constructive criticism.[10] Saul failed to deal openly and fairly with David. He made dysfunctional choices from which he could never recover.

In describing how a business can be a center of excellence, Dieter Frey, Eva Jonas, and Tobias Greitemeyer stated, "To achieve top performance as a global player in the international market, all employees must have a high achievement ethos, must constantly learn and improve processes, and must show responsibility and courage."[11] Sounds a lot like David, doesn't it?

Saul became even more determined to finish David off. So David learned a lot about life on the run. He also learned to run into his heavenly Father's arms. David penned Psalm 142 while hiding in a cave. Verses 5-7 record David's prayer: "You are my refuge, my portion in the land of the living. Attend to my cry, For I am brought very low; Deliver me from my persecutors, For they are stronger than I. Bring my soul out of prison, That I may praise Your name; The righteous shall surround me, For You shall deal bountifully with me." (NKJV) David found his strength and courage through his trust in the Lord.[12]

At one point in Saul's pursuit of him, David crept forward from his hiding place in a cave and cut off a piece of Saul's robe. When Saul was away from the cave, David yelled to him, showing him the piece of robe. David was trying in every way to show Saul that he still respected him as king, regardless of how abysmally Saul had treated him. Unfortunately, this did not deter the tyrant.

King Saul took Michal way and gave her to another man. I guess back then women didn't have much say in such matters!

David and his band of men ran into a surly man named Nabal. Nabal was quite rude to David and his men, but Nabal's wife, Abigail, was very wise. She took gifts to David and thereby kept the peace. David was so impressed that he later married her.[13] Unfortunately, this started the destructive practice of his taking more than one wife, which was an evil God had warned him against.[14]

Saul went on a rampage to find David again. This time, while Saul and his men slept, David bravely crept into the camp with a friend and stole Saul's spear and water jug. David showed the articles the next day in an effort to convince Saul he meant Saul no harm. Saul apologized and headed home.

But David knew the apology wouldn't last. *One of these days*, David thought, *Saul will destroy me*. In his exhaustion, he began to attack anyone who might talk to Saul about him. So he slaughtered the innocent people of Gath.[15] God had not told David to do this and He did not condone the shedding of innocent blood. It is imperative to lean solely on the Lord to guide our actions.[16]

Meanwhile, Saul had resorted to consulting mediums about his future. The mediums summoned Samuel from the dead. Annoyed at being bothered, Samuel informed Saul that the kingdom would be taken out of his hands and given to David.[17]

Just as Samuel had predicted, the Philistines destroyed Saul and his three sons. Saul took his own spear and fell upon it.[18] When David and his men returned to Israel and found out what had happened, they mourned, wept, and tore their clothes.[19]

In his grief, David remembered Saul and Jonathan with great love. He exclaimed, "Saul and Jonathan – in life they were loved and gracious, and in death they were not parted. They were swifter than eagles, they were stronger than lions." (2 Samuel 1:23 NIV)

David added, "I grieve for you, Jonathan my brother, you were very dear to me. Your love for me was wonderful, more wonderful than that of women." (2 Samuel 1:26 NIV)

David officially became king. He danced through the streets in jubilation when he brought the ark of God to Jerusalem. (see 2 Samuel 6:14-15)

Folly occurred, however, when he took many wives and concubines. This may have been acceptable in those times, but it was not acceptable in God's sight.

At this time, the prophet Nathan emerged as David's advisor. God told Nathan in a dream that David's house would endure forever before God. (see 2 Samuel 7:16) And David ruled justly over all the people. (see 2 Samuel 8:15)

Eventually, however, David began to shirk his duty. He stayed at home when he should have been leading his men on the battlefield.[20] One night he saw beautiful Bathsheba bathing on her roof, and summoned her to his quarters. They began an affair. Bathsheba became pregnant with David's child.[21]

In an attempt to cover his sin, David ordered Bathsheba's husband, Uriah, home from the battlefield. Uriah, ever loyal to his troops, refused to sleep with his wife. His heart was with his men in battle. And so David compounded his sin by having Uriah placed at the front of the battle lines so he would be killed.[22]

Using evocative language and intense storytelling, the prophet Nathan set the stage to convict David of his terrible crimes against God and Uriah. Nathan appealed to the king's imagination to lead David to the ultimate, horrible truth of what he had done.

Rather than coming right out and stating the fact that David slept with Uriah's wife, Bathsheba, and then had Uriah killed to cover up the pregnancy which resulted from this adultery, Nathan skillfully approached the king with a moving allegory.

Nathan told about a rich sheep-owner and a poor man who had but one sheep. Nathan described the bereft man in detail; "And the very poor, owning nothing but a little lamb he had managed to buy. It was his children's pet and he fed it from his own plate and let it drink from his own cup; he cuddled it in his arms like a baby daughter." (2 Samuel 12:3)

When Nathan explained that the rich man took the poor man's lamb and roasted it and served it up to guests, he succeeded in raising David's great ire. Such a man, declared David, should be put to death. Now the boom was lowered. Can't you see Nathan point straight at the king as he declared, "*You* are that rich man"? It is as if Nathan was holding up a mirror to David. The image was ugly.

Nathan gave David a good dressing down. He laid out all the marvelous things God had done for David and all the great opportunities He had given to David. Through Nathan, God asked, "Why, then, have you despised God's laws and done this horrible deed?" What could David say? Indeed, what can you or I say when the prophet's mirror is held up to us?

Next, God delineated David's punishment. Staggering repercussions resulted from David's brutal actions. His household was rebellious, and his wives went to bed with other men. Worst of all, the child he had conceived with Bathsheba did not survive. (see 2 Samuel 12:14)

The writer of 2 Samuel reports that David went without food and lay all night praying for the child's survival. Once the baby died, however, David accepted God's will, got up, and went about his business. (see 2 Samuel 22-23)

He returned to his proper role as leader of the army. He led the attack on Rabbah. To his credit, he made a fantastic comeback. Yes, he had made some very poor choices. But he recovered by going back to doing the things he should have been doing all long.

And then, at last, with Nathan's blessing, Bathsheba bore David a son. His name was Solomon, and he became the wisest man who ever lived.

And so we see ourselves in David's story. Haven't we all, over the vantage point of many years of maturity, looked back with a sick heart on some of the things we have done? Perhaps the Holy Spirit brings those things to our remembrance. We, like David, must repent. We must accept divine chastisement. We must wear our sackcloth and ashes.

But then we must arise. God forgave David; He will forgive us too. In His great mercy, He sent His perfect Son to take the full punishment we deserved. After a personal failure, we must recover and begin again to do that special, distinct work God has for us to do.

David's story can inspire us to have the strength to try again. Something that might drive a person out of his mind can be buffered and overcome by banking on strengths such as faith and courage.[23] With Christ's help, we can seize the courage to do what we could never do alone.

Even years after God has forgiven us for a sin we may still be dealing with the natural consequences accompanying that sin. David's household was replete with siblings, half-siblings, and the offspring of his concubines. All of David's sexual relationships must have been confusing to his children.

Amnon, David's eldest, plotted and schemed until he was able to get Tamar, his virginal half-sister, alone. Then he raped her.[24] This wicked act not only destroyed Tamar's life, it also led her brother, Absalom, on a path of wild vengeance. Absalom waited two years for David to punish Amnon. King David did not do so. So Absalom had his half-brother killed.[25] He hid out for three years and then waited two more years in Jerusalem for David to receive him. He never gleaned satisfaction. Hence he spent the next four years plotting vengeance against his father.

When Absalom won David's highly respected adviser, Ahithophel, to his side, David responded by running.[26] Where was his trust in the God who had made him king? Where was the courage he had shown when he killed Goliath?

Finally, David's army battled the rebellious men who had sided with Absalom. David could not help but tell his men to be careful concerning Absalom. (see 2 Samuel 18:5) Nevertheless, Absalom was killed. David wept bitterly. He wished he could have died rather than his precious son.

His grief was crippling.[27]

The pain and suffering David experienced throughout his life began to catch up with him. He became old and weak. There was just one last act to complete. Nathan, the prophet, told Bathsheba that Haggith's son Adonijhah was trying to seize the kingdom. Bathsheba told David, reminding him that it was her son, Solomon, who had been promised the throne. David decreed that Solomon would be the next king to sit upon the throne.[28] And so he was.

First Chronicles 29: 26-28 summed up, "David was king of the land of Israel for forty years; seven of them during his reign in Hebron and thirty-three in Jerusalem. He died at an old age, wealthy and honored; and his son Solomon reigned in his place."

David's ability to protect Israel led to his divine appointment as the king over God's chosen people. Being a man after God's own heart, David dreamed of building a magnificent temple to honor his Lord. He commissioned Solomon, his son, to do the work, saying, "Every part of this blueprint was given to me in writing from the hand of the Lord…Be strong and courageous and get to work. Don't be frightened by the size of the task for the Lord, my God, is with you. He will not forsake you." (1 Chronicles 28:19-20)

The same mandate applies to each of us. You never know what important work He will accomplish in your life if you ask Him to tell you what to do. He will answer you. When you feel His directing and prompting, take courage and move toward achieving your God-given dream with passion and diligence. Be secure in the fact that the outcome rests in His hands and that all the glory belongs to Him.

Just as Solomon faced the monumental task of building the temple David envisioned to give glory to God, the tasks ahead of you may seem overwhelming. Take comfort; God will be beside you every step of the way. Just keep taking small steps toward your ultimate goals. Head in the right direction, and just put one foot in front of the other. Bravery is attainable when it is broken into doable parts.

Throughout his life, David exemplified the spiritual practice of emptying himself of his fears and realizing the battle was not his but the Lord's. Are you, like David, building an active history with the Lord? David believed with all his heart that God was with him, and so had the courage to trust that his daunting mission would succeed.

God has a mission for each of us – a special individually designed destiny. You can step out in faith and bravely ask God what that mission is. Wait with expectancy until He provides the answers.

Throughout history, great leaders have emerged with God-given visions that changed the world. Martin Luther King, Jr. worked nonviolently to create opportunities and equality for African Americans. FDR put the people of America back to work and pulled the country out of the Great Depression.

When God gives someone a vision, He also gives that person the passion, focus, and unwavering motivation to achieve that vision. He gives the tools necessary for the seeker to fulfill his or her mission. Courage is a crucial tool for success. There is a close relationship between courage and hope.

Three basic elements help us enlarge our understanding of bravery; valor, diligence, and integrity. We display valor when we face challenge, pain, or difficulty without shrinking.[29] Think of Jesus' quiet strength as He prayed in the Garden of Gethsemane, where He sweat great drops of blood. Asking the Father to remove the cup from Him (His impending crucifixion), He prayed, "Not My will, but Thine be done." Courage is often affiliated with asserting one's own will, but we see in the Gethsemane experience that true courage is relinquishing our will to the heavenly Father.

No matter how difficult the circumstance, Christ never lost His dignity. Much of being courageous consists of taking a stoic and even cheerful stance needed to face serious ordeals and persistent suffering without loss of dignity. When we adopt Christ's mind, we develop the ever-growing ability to deal with difficulties with patience. When we seek to find and do His will, the Lord will cover and protect our dignity.

One of the biggest difficulties many believers face is that of accepting responsibility for past failures. As we learned from studying David's life, there is no escaping the consequences of our actions. It is a valiant act to face past wrongs squarely and change our ways. It may spare our loved ones and us years of additional pain. It is never too late to take responsibility and make a new start. The only truly fatal mistake is that of giving up.

Diligence is the ability to refuse to give up, to finish what we start, and to wait with expectancy on the Lord's power. When we possess this ability, we do what we say we will do and deliver what we had promised or even more. Of course, we must lean on Jesus for the strength to be diligent. Also, we must take care not to expect ourselves to be perfect.

We can overcome the self-defeating thoughts and behavior of perfectionism by employing our courage. The important thing to remember is that there is a crucial difference between setting high standards versus perfectionistic ideals. This means having the clarity to set modest goals.

Learn how to talk to yourself about keeping things reasonable. Don't be overly critical of your abilities or how you look. Having a nice appearance is different from obsessing in front of the mirror. Realize that competing and comparing are futile and destructive endeavors. Find out what you are best at and then make a realistic goal based on that attribute.[30] Strive to remain flexible, realistic, and industrious.[31]

Matthew 25: 14-30 taught about the virtue of industriousness. This illustration focuses on a master who left his residence and entrusted his money with three servants. Two of the servants took cautious risks and invested their money. They made profits on the money under their care. Unfortunately, the perfectionistic fearful servant buried his treasure in a hole because he was paralyzed by fear of failure or disappointing his master. Can you relate?

When the master returned, he gave greater responsibilities to the servants who had made profits, whereas he did not entrust the fearful servant with further responsibility. Just as the master expected his servants to grow the resources he had given them, so God believes we should use the gifts He has bestowed on us. All that is required is that we make a reasonable attempt to do something useful with our abilities so they will bear fruit. It does, however, involve taking some degree of risk.

An anonymous Chicago teacher wrote eloquently about how being a person of integrity entailed certain risks:

To laugh is to risk appearing the fool.

To weep is to risk appearing sentimental.

To reach for another is to risk involvement.

To expose your feelings is to risk exposing your true self.

To place your ideas, your dreams before a crowd, is to risk their loss.

To love is to risk not being loved in return.

To live is to risk dying.

To believe is to risk despair.

To try is to risk failure.

But risks must be taken

Because the greatest hazard in life is to risk nothing.

This teacher spoke with a great deal of integrity. Integrity involves not only speaking the truth but also living in an authentic and genuine manner. It means letting down our pretense and being real.[32]

These attributes do not magically appear because we wish to possess them. Courage, like any virtue, is similar to a muscle. You can possess more of any virtue through practice. With dedication, courage can take root and flourish.

My husband, David, is a big fan of University of Kentucky basketball. He receives their publication, *The Cat's Pause*. He excitedly showed me the August 2009 issue. "I have the perfect story for your book that exemplifies courage,' he exclaimed. The article talked about the life of Orlando Antigua. Antigua was made an assistant basketball coach at UK in April 2009.

From humble beginnings, Antigua has overcome many challenges to become the success he is today. He cites his grandmother's prayers as pivotal to his achievements over the years.

Antigua was born into poverty in the Dominican Republic. His mom left his two brothers and him there while she made her way to the Bronx to give her family a better life. As soon as there was enough money, the boys joined her.

He is well positioned to help his players overcome obstacles because he himself overcame so many. Some of those included living on streets where drugs and violence were rampant. He avoided this life by finding a group of friends who played stickball, baseball, and basketball.

In addition to being homeless for a time, he was shot as an innocent bystander on the mean streets of the Bronx. The bullet hit near his left eye. He could have died. Fortunately, it lodged in his left ear and was safely extracted later.

Some good things were happening to him at that time too. In the eighth grade, Antigua shot up to 6'5". He was awarded a scholarship to Raymond's High School for Boys. After becoming senior class president and receiving the courage award from the U.S. Basketball Association, Antigua wrangled a scholarship to the University of Pittsburgh. While there he scored nine hundred points and four hundred rebounds. He stayed on at the university another semester to complete the degree as he had promised his mother he would.

With his degree behind him, Orlando went to play with the Harlem Globetrotters. He was the first Hispanic to do so. He stayed with them for several years, traveling all over the world. The story explained, "He performed on the David Letterman show, matched basketball skills with Magic Johnson, and shook the hand of Nelson Mandela, the Nobel Prize winner who was imprisoned for twenty-eight years for opposing South Africa's apartheid policy."[33]

Antigua pursued another challenging opportunity as an assistant coach at the University of Kentucky. His mandate? To help others reach their dreams. Antigua put it this way: "God is the only one who can save your life. Basketball allowed me to live life. It has allowed us to better our circumstances, see the world, and make a living off something I absolutely love. Basketball has allowed me to live my life and my dream."[34]

Orlando Antigua is a perfect illustration of a person who succeeded by internalizing vital character strengths like courage. Character traits can be compared to fruit; to be of quality they must ripen gradually.

So how do we ensure that we grow to flourish and bear good fruit – what we have been placed on Planet Earth to accomplish? The only no-fail manner in which to assure that we produce the fruit we are supposed to is to stay grafted to our source for all good things, including life itself. We must realize who we are in relation to Jesus and His Father. In John 15:5 Jesus promised, "I am the Vine, you are the branches. Whoever lives in me and I in him shall produce a large crop of fruit."

If we study the Word and pray regularly, we will acquire Christ's mind. Staying connected to the Vine means our joy will overflow and Jesus will call us His friends. (John 15:6-14) Being Jesus' friends will give us a great deal of security. It will help us to believe in things not yet seen. It will help us to be positive in a negative situation. It will allow us to trust that God will ultimately work out every suffering and trial for our good.

Courage is being willing to change and take moderate risks. It is about not hesitating to move ahead with the plans the Lord has revealed to you. Passion and motivation are necessary if you are to reach your full potential. As you work hard on the projects that you care about and are interested in, your ability in those areas will increase.[35]

As the cowardly lion was required to reach inside to find the best that was within him, you can find the courage to become an unwavering believer. Glorifying and honoring the great and mighty living God is critical to success.

In Leviticus 22:31-33, God admonished, "You must not treat Me as common and ordinary. Revere Me and hallow Me, for I, the Lord, made you holy to Myself and rescued you from Egypt to be My own people. I am Jehovah."

The only way to effectively be a courageous person is to have a heart for the Lord. He wants you to love and honor Him with all your heart, mind, and soul. When you do all you can, and then cast your care on the Lord, you can be assured He will not forsake you. Have the courage within to live out your purpose fully and achieve all God designed. For He determined your destiny when He formed you in the seclusion of your mother's womb.

6 PERSEVERANCE: NEVER GIVE UP

"Take the old prophets as your mentors. They put up with anything, went through everything, and never once quit, all the time honoring God. What a gift life is to those who stay the course!" (James 5: 10 Message)

Are you completing your most important goals? It takes perseverance to do so. Perseverance is an aptitude that can be either natural or acquired. By *acquired* I mean it can be learned.

Perseverance means refusing to give up. Or, said another way, it is having the willingness to try again after losing or quitting. James 5:10 instructed us to use the old prophets as our examples. In this chapter, you will have the opportunity to examine the life of Nehemiah, a successful leader who persevered to the end.

An attitude is a manner of carrying oneself. Would you like to carry yourself with the persevering leadership style Nehemiah exhibited? What an adventure he had in completing his mission! The same can be true for you.

Leading and persevering are strengths you can build like muscles. Jesus will help you if you ask Him. Whatever challenges you are facing, with Christ's help, you can reach higher ground. In this way, you can help others and glorify God with your service. It is amazing what can happen if you stay the course and take the risk of being responsible for the completion of your God-given mission.

Simply put, perseverance is the art of finishing what you start. It means taking on challenging projects and finishing them with, as Martin Seligman phrased it, "good cheer and minimal complaints."[1] The persevering person is flexible and realistic, and delivers what is promised without getting into the dysfunction of perfectionism.

Dr. Seligman also said in *Learned Optimism* that success is more than having the aptitude to complete a project. He commented, "Success requires persistence, the ability to not give up in the face of failure."[2] He concluded that this persistence can occur when a person explains things to himself or herself in an optimistic style. He defines three characteristics necessary for ongoing success: aptitude, motivation, and optimism.[3]

John Maxwell speaks and writes about success to the corporate business world as well as to the Christian community. "Leadership truly develops from the inside out. If you can become the leader you ought to be on the inside, you will be able to become the leader you want to be on the outside. People will want to follow you. And when this happens, you'll be able to tackle anything in this world," he says.[4]

What could be more exciting than trying to make the world a better place? Can you capitalize on your strengths to effect change both within and beyond yourself? Like perseverance, leadership is an aptitude you can grow into. It is an attitude that says; with God's help, I can, you can, and we can.

One of the most astute decisions you can make as a leader is to help your employees discover their unused signature strengths. Let's say you supervise a group of lawyers. All of them possess prudence and high verbal intelligence, but each has distinct strengths that if used on a side project could really energize the productivity of each individual.[5]

There was a certain African tribe was a puzzle to anthropologists. For hundreds of years this tribe enjoyed a 100 percent success rate with its rain dance. Other tribes did similar rain dances but did not always experience success. Their rituals, their costumes, and their methods of praying were all the same. Finally, someone discovered the truth behind this mystery. While all the tribes at times danced continually for days and even weeks, the tribe with total success refused to stop dancing until the rains came. That's perseverance!

Boredom and anxiety can lead to giving up. But if a person is working in one of his or her strength areas and can get into flow, those negative attributes can abate. Flow occurs when both the challenge and the skills to meet the challenge are at above-average levels. When a person experiences flow, he or she is encouraged to persevere. In fact, there is a relationship between persistence and the quality of the worker's experience. Time spent in flow can improve self-esteem. Mastering the challenges of living can act as a buffer against negative outcomes.[6]

Perseverance is an essential quality for those of us who hope to lead others to Christ. It is also a key to being effective in the body of Christ.

The book of Nehemiah provided an example of a man on a mission who possessed the vision and ability to set goals which led to his ultimate success. Nehemiah had a specific and formidable task – to rebuild the broken-down wall around Jerusalem.

When Nehemiah first heard about the wall's devastation, he sat and wept.[7] He cared. First and foremost, leaders must care.

After drying his tears, Nehemiah took action. He did not start by writing his "to do" list. He did not make a grand announcement about the terrible state of the wall around Jerusalem. He did not immediately jump into action. No, he got on his knees and prayed.[8]

He began by putting first things first. His first act was to seek out God's direction. Repeatedly, throughout his story, Nehemiah slipped away in solitude. He beseeched God to show him His will. Because of Nehemiah's devotion to God, the workers under his leadership completed the wall of Jerusalem in an incredible fifty-two days.[9]

Nehemiah was wise enough to think clearly and pursue goals that would lead to ultimate fulfillment for his people rather than chasing goals that would give only the illusion of fulfillment. Wisdom is displayed when a person pursues positively framed goals that are good for the collective in a prudent, patient, and persevering manner.[10] Nehemiah moved forward in just such a way.

The book of Nehemiah was written as an autobiography. Nehemiah discovered that the wall of Jerusalem was in a state of total disrepair. He wept and fasted for several days. He cried out to God and reminded Him of the words He had spoken to Moses: "If you sin, I will scatter you among the nations; but if you return to me and obey laws, even though you are exiled to the farthest corners of the universe, I will bring you back to Jerusalem. For Jerusalem is the place in which I have chosen to live." (Nehemiah 1: 8-9)

After confessing the Israelites' sins, Nehemiah reminded the Lord of His promises.[11] This is a great prescription for us today. When we go to God and repent, and then remind Him of His own words and promises, He can move miraculously in our circumstances.

At the time God convicted Nehemiah to lead the rebuilding of Jerusalem's wall, Nehemiah was serving as the cupbearer to King Artaxerxes of Persia. As a cupbearer, he was very close to the king. His job was to test the king's food and drink to determine whether it was safe.

Nehemiah prayed that God would give the king a kind heart for the task he desired to accomplish. Then he waited – for four months.[12]

One of the things I would most like to emulate about Nehemiah is his habit of praying seriously for long periods before he undertook any action. This encourages me to talk to God about everything. I don't have to use fancy language; I just need to communicate in intimacy with my Maker. Then He will certainly guide my steps. It is vital to check with God before beginning a project to make sure it is His will and not just something I myself take on.

One day as he was serving the king his wine, the king noticed Nehemiah was troubled, and asked why. This was Nehemiah's opportunity to share what had been on his heart. He fearfully asked the king to send him home to rebuild Jerusalem. The king's immediate response was simply, "How long will you be gone?"[13] God moved the king's heart to grant Nehemiah's request.

Chapter two of Nehemiah featured him in Jerusalem. As a wise builder, Nehemiah proceeded cautiously. This habit was perhaps the secret to much of his success. When he arrived in Jerusalem, he realized the time was not right to tell anyone he was going to rebuild Jerusalem's wall. Instead, he waited until nightfall to inspect the state of the wall. As he toured the wall by horseback, he saw the rubble was too high to access in many areas.

This moonlit excursion allowed Nehemiah to assess the situation accurately. He then had a good idea of his project's scope. He knew it was going to be challenging and rigorous.

At the right time, Nehemiah approached the city officials. He explained, "You know full well the tragedy of our city; it lies in ruins and its gates are burned. Let us rebuild the wall of Jerusalem and rid ourselves of this disgrace." (Nehemiah 2:17)

After Nehemiah had thoroughly diagnosed the problem, he took an active role in solving it. He did not sit back and tell city officials what they should do – he joined in. He suggested they rebuild the wall together. If you and I wish to make this world a better place, we too must do more than tell others what to do. We need to join in the labor and encourage our associates – we must be willing to get our hands dirty.

Nehemiah was successful in creating a team ready to work together. The officials agreed to begin the work at once. Rebuilding the entire wall of Jerusalem was a daunting task. Nehemiah prudently divided the work and assigned different parts of the wall to different groups. This greatly helped make the overwhelming nature of the task less frightening and more feasible. That's what leaders do; they inspire those they supervise by breaking up jobs into small, doable steps.

Even so, the challenges were not over for Nehemiah. Enemies rose up to oppose the successful rebuilding of the wall. Sanballat and Tobiah ridiculed him.[14] Isn't it encouraging that Nehemiah endured their sarcasm and persisted in the task set before him? Sometimes when people treat us poorly we want to throw up our hands and give up. We can learn from Nehemiah's example. He chose simply to keep his focus on God rather than on the ridicule. Christ made this same choice while He agonizingly hung on the cross to take the punishment for our sins.

Nehemiah's story shows us the importance of choosing to concentrate and focus on the right thing. Despite great odds and enemies, Nehemiah and his people completed the wall. With God's help, the group achieved in two months a job that had been left undone for a hundred years.

Nehemiah is a great role model. He was willing to lead by example. He sacrificed his own rights for the good of the people. If we can forget ourselves and persevere, letting nothing turn us from our purpose, we can join Nehemiah in saying, "I am doing a great work!" Seek God for clear direction. You have a calling no less important than Nehemiah's.

The optimistic person perseveres. Such optimism helps when the work gets hard.[15] When we persevere, we inspire others. Martin Seligman tells a story about his home-schooled son, Darryl, that humorously drives this point home. Darryl, who had a rock collection, accompanied a mineralogist to collect specimens. After hours of collecting, Darryl was urged back to the car. "Darryl, sweaty and dirty and sitting on top of a huge pile of rocks at a construction site, shouted back, 'Mineralogists don't take breaks,'" Seligman wrote.[16]

An admirer once exclaimed to Theodore Roosevelt, "Mr. Roosevelt, you are a great man." Roosevelt responded, "No, Teddy Roosevelt is simply a plain, ordinary man – highly motivated."[17]

Think of people who are good at putting puzzles together. While others give up after making a good effort, the skilled puzzle player knows he or she has all the pieces of the whole on the table. It is just a matter of finding out which piece fits where. Once the person can do that, the puzzle is complete. As Vic Johnson explains, "Putting a piece in the wrong place is not a cause for concern; it is simply another step toward putting all of the pieces in their proper place."[18]

A study of salespeople revealed that those who tested optimistic kept improving over those who tested pessimistic. Why did this happen? It became evident that optimism mattered because it produced perseverance. It was hypothesized before the experiment that talent and motivation would be as important to success as perseverance. As time went on and things got tough, it was those salespeople who persevered who did the best.[19]

It is interesting to notice Nehemiah did not retire immediately after completing his big project. He became the people's governor.[20] He devised a plan for guarding the wall. He also created a system to register all who had returned to Jerusalem now that its borders were secure.

Then Nehemiah did what is often the hardest thing of all for a leader – he handed the authority to someone better qualified for the next steps in God's desire for Jerusalem: Ezra.[21]

Nehemiah knew Ezra possessed the skills to lead the Jewish people to revival. He was happy his organizational skills had created a safe boundary for Jerusalem. Now the people were ready to grow in spiritual maturity.

In *Hand Me Another Brick*, Charles Swindoll said, "Tucked away in the old book of Nehemiah is the first recorded revival."[22] Ezra read to the people out of the scroll of Moses' laws. The people bowed with their faces to the ground and worshiped the Lord. As they came to understand what Ezra was reading, all the people sobbed.

Then Ezra and Nehemiah instructed the people not to cry. "Don't cry on such a day as this! For today is a sacred day before the Lord you God –it is time to celebrate with a hearty meal and to send presents to those in need, for the joy of the Lord is your strength. You must not be dejected and sad." (Nehemiah 8:9-10)

The people participated in a seven-day feast. On the eighth day, there was a solemn closing – the people came together again to fast and clothe themselves in sackcloth. They sprinkled dirt on themselves. Ezra recounted the relationship God and His people should have. Then the religious leaders formalized a pact to be accountable to God. The people agreed to be obedient.

Positive psychology at the group level rests on institutions that move people toward better citizenship. Some of the attributes that help a collective thrive are responsibility, nurturance, altruism, civility, moderation, tolerance, and work ethic.[23]

Systematically, groups of Israelites returned to live in Jerusalem. There were now heathy boundaries of protection. The people held an ecstatic ceremony to dedicate the city wall. It turned out to be the happiest event Israel had experienced in more than half a century! It is amazing how happy we, God's people, become after we repent of our sins and renew our obedience to our awesome Creator and Sustainer.

With everything looking good, Nehemiah returned to his job under King Artaxerxes. However, it wasn't long before Nehemiah again needed permission to return to Jerusalem. He had heard that a temple storeroom had been made into a beautiful guestroom for a man who was not only not a Jew but also an enemy to the Jews' cause. Nehemiah angrily threw out the man's belongings and restored the space to its original purpose. He insisted that the people give the Levite priests their fair wage. He also swiftly put an end to any work that was being conducted on the Sabbath. Further, he forcefully prohibited marriage to the heathen. Isn't it predictable that even after a great revival and a declaration of obedience to God that the people fell into sin again? Aren't they just so typically human? Can't you relate to their failure?

Leadership duties do not end after a mountaintop experience. When a prudent leader faces the fact that sin has reemerged among the group, he does not throw up his hands in disgust. He, like Nehemiah, must once again step boldly forward to put things back into their proper order.

Nehemiah showed himself to be an effective leader. He kept his focus on achieving specific goals without losing sight of "the big picture." He could see the results of his "now" ahead of time.[24] He influenced and organized his people so they might have all God had prepared for them. We should do no less.

Nehemiah did not entertain a self-serving agenda. He had a servant's heart. He understood that a person becomes an adult when he or she realizes that life is not about what you get, but rather about what you give. When you are motivated by intrinsic rewards rather than self-centered ones, you can use your curiosity and persistence to accomplish much.[25]

God never sends His leaders into any situation with a faulty plan or a plan to fail. If we are following God's desires, we will succeed mightily. We must always be aware to move forth God's agenda and His objectives, no more and no less. There is no place for ego in servant leadership. Think about your leadership in your home, your workplace, and your church. Are you aware that one of the stamps of great leaders is they spend much of their time training their successors?

The supreme example of this was Jesus' lengthy training program for His disciples. Think of the great selflessness of the greatest Self ever to grace the earth! Jesus successfully faced the powerful and universal temptations with which every leader must grapple. He did not need recognition or applause. He did not lust for power or use it improperly. He never pursued self-gratification.

He knew who He was. He knew without a doubt who His Father was. He never failed to obey God's Word. He knew the Word intimately. He was free of pride and just as free of fear. He knew very well what Proverbs 29:25 said, "Fearing people is a dangerous trap, but trusting the LORD means safety."

Trusting in the Lord means never putting something else in His place as the object of our worship. It means never relying on sources other than Him for our security. Trusting in the Lord means staying in intimate communion with Him and resting in His unconditional love.

If the devil had a formula for self-worth it would be as follows: your self-worth is equal to your performance plus the opinions of others.[26] We demonstrate our trust in the Lord by putting our self-worth securely and completely in His hands. He is our Abba. We must grasp this truth. It is God who created us. It is God who determines our destiny. It is God to whom we will someday return. Selah. Ponder that.

We are not here to fulfill our own purposes. God created us to fit into His purposes. I need to realize I am not here to fulfill my plans for my life. God created me to fulfill His plans for me. If I don't fall into line with God's will for my life, I miss the best He has for me. What a waste my God-given life will have been if it has not been God-directed. How sad it would be if we did not trust Him enough to confidently carry out the work He has for us.

My friend Lorna was told by her high school guidance counselor that she was not college material. Frustrated, she graduated after the first half of her senior year and went to work at a pizza place. Soon she was the manager. Eventually she put her experiences on the high school newspaper staff to good use and applied for a job working at a magazine that deals with antique guns. She got the job and before you know it she was Director of Publications. She has successfully managed the magazine for many years. She took the raw intelligence and leadership ability she had and made the most of it.

The cornerstones of positive psychology are having commitment and confidence that foster perseverance even in the face of great adversity. It means having a goal that matters, one to which you will commit fully. It also means having the confidence that you *will* eventually achieve your goal, no matter how difficult.[27] It is pursing the goal, as Nehemiah did, with ferocious fearlessness.

The only fear we should have is a healthy fear of the Lord. Psalm 111:10 stated that the fear of the Lord is the beginning of wisdom. When we faithfully trust in God's complete love for us, we push fear and pride out of our lives and leave no room for anything but His love.

In John 13:12-17, we see God's unconditional love embodied in the acts of Jesus Christ. He was our perfect and outstanding example of a servant leader. Just before the Last Supper, He knelt to wash the disciples' feet.

Jesus asked, "Do you know what I have done to you? You call Me teacher and Lord, and you say well, for so I am. If I then, your Lord and Teacher, have washed your feet, you also ought to wash one another's feet. For I have given you an example, that you should do as I have done to you. Most assuredly, I say to you, a servant is not greater than his master; nor is he who is sent greater than he who sent him. If you know these things, blessed are you if you do them." (John 13: 12-17 NKJV)

How can you incorporate the act of "washing the feet" of those in your life? Do you really believe that the servant who gives is happier than the person who takes? How have you seen this play out in your life and the lives of others?

Examine the events that led to Jesus' crucifixion. In His dying, He saved all believers. He persevered through every challenge presented to Him. He kept reaching out to the crowds while training a small band of disciples in love and intimacy.

As Nehemiah returned home to rebuild the wall, so people today return to rebuild their homes in war-torn territories. "The ability of people to struggle forward, to persevere against great odds even in the face of failure, represents a very important human strength," said Carver and Scheier in *A Psychology of Human Strengths*.[28]

Let us, as instructed, follow Jesus and take up our cross. He beckons, "My yoke is easy and My burden is light." (Matthew 11:30 NKJV)

In *A Leader in the Making*, Joyce Meyer pointed out that joining with others in our endeavors boosts our endurance. We certainly see this truth portrayed in Nehemiah's life. Meyer expounded, "God does not have to anoint anything He does not tell us to do."[29]

This means we must be earnest in following Nehemiah's example of much prayer and preparation before action. We must wait patiently for God's still, small voice.

Learn to be a God-pleaser rather than a people-pleaser. As Hebrews 12:2 tells us, Jesus is "the author and the finisher." (KJV) Let us be diligent in completing that which He has begun in us. If we allow Him, He certainly will bring our efforts to fruition…and we will thrive.

7 WHAT WILL YOUR STORY BE?

I hope that you found the preceding chapters inspiring. Perhaps there are elements from the stories of the Biblical heroes that you can incorporate into your own story.

As demonstrated by Abraham in chapter two, it is not strenuous moral striving that makes us right with God. Peace with God comes from our trusting faith in Him and what He can accomplish with our lives if we put them into His loving hands. We can believe every promise He made in His Word. Those promises are for you and for me if we will only believe.

The central message of the Scriptures is the fact that Christ died for our sins so that we might spend eternity with Him. Because of that great sacrifice, you can come before God at any time. He will hear you and He will help you. He is always there to listen and respond.

Deep within you there exists the same intensity of faith that God found in Abraham. Through our Savior, we who are Christians became the spiritual descendants of Abraham.

Because Abraham resolutely obeyed Him, God promised to bless him and make him famous. God stated that Abraham would be a blessing to many others.

Likewise, by wholeheartedly trusting in God, you, too, can enjoy a blessed life. You, too, can be a blessing to many others. In the final analysis, what could be more rewarding than that?

Just as Abraham and Sarah birthed Isaac many years after they were beyond childbearing years, so it is never too late for you to birth great things in your life. All it takes is faith in Jesus.

Abraham was so obedient to God that he was willing to sacrifice his precious son when God asked him to. God spared Isaac at the last moment. God did not spare His own son, however, from dying a painful death on the cross to make salvation possible for you and for me.

All this is not to say that Abraham was perfect. Far from it. His dumb moves can be reassuring to us as we make our own inevitable mistakes. His fearful attempts to pass his wife off as his sister to two rulers who found her beautiful were patently foolish. Perhaps his stupidest act was to impregnate Hagar instead of waiting to conceive the child God had promised with his wife. Hence, the offspring of Abraham's sons, Isaac and Ishmael, have battled fiercely until this very day.

God loves us even in our sinfulness, just as He loved Abraham. Certainly it is vital to wait on God's timing. But thankfully, a poor performance cannot negate His plan for our lives if we keep trusting Him for guidance.

God is supremely compassionate and powerful. There is no mistake we make that He cannot correct if we sincerely ask Him to. The Almighty can make Plan B better than Plan A would have ever been. Never give up. Only believe. He can make every promise for your life a reality.

Will you, like Joshua and Caleb, be strong and courageous in the face of difficulties? If so, like them, you will need to study the Bible persistently – meditating on it day and night. I'll admit I have my share of fearful thoughts. It is comforting to be given an effective and simple strategy for success – read the Bible.

There is a very good reason not to be fearful nor demoralized – as believers, Emmanuel is with us wherever we go. It doesn't get any better than that. This gives us a valid reason to be optimistic. Joshua knew the source of his optimism – an all-powerful, loving, and creative God.

To be honest, confidence is sometimes difficult for me. But it becomes a viable option when I realize that true self-assurance occurs when I trust wholeheartedly, not in myself, but in God. When we turn our lives completely over to the Lord and cast our cares upon Him, He will take care of us and help us live up to our full potential.

Joshua and Caleb were able to trust God fully. Even when they had to take the minority position, they chose to believe that the Lord would do exactly what He promised. They knew that God was much more powerful than any other force.

Optimism gives us hope. It can help us make positive changes and set realistic goals. It can encourage us to take the steps necessary to make our most heartfelt dreams come to pass.

God is optimistic about your life. Perhaps it comes as a surprise to fully realize that He wants you to feel respected and loved. His acceptance is all you really need.

His care can give you the strength and courage to meet any challenge you might face. Like Joshua and Caleb, you too can get into the Promised Land, if you will only believe.

Accentuating our strengths without ignoring our weaknesses engenders "flexible optimism." The plasticity of our brains makes it possible for us to choose to be more optimistic on purpose.

Most of us are not very good at picking out what will make us happy. This is a very good reason not to independently run our own lives. It is much wiser to put ourselves in God's capable hands.

Optimism and humor have a positive relationship. Laughing is so good for us physically and emotionally. It is needed more than ever in this day and age in which greatly increasing numbers of people suffer from depression.

Depression and learned helplessness go hand in hand – the feelings of being trapped without options, and believing that defeat is inevitable. Rather than believing you are helpless, have faith that with God's assistance you can change your life. Refuse to catastrophize your situation. Look at things realistically. Setbacks are temporary when you choose to become for yourself rather than against.

Being for yourself and others means you are willing to forgive. Forgiveness is embodied through radical kindness. Even when you are discouraged remember that you do have strengths and abilities. Embrace them – particularly in the tough times. Don't abandon your life to the enemy. Hold you head up high and claim the future God has ordained.

Forgiveness is the miraculous gift that can help you let go and be free. Gandhi once said that, "The weak can never forgive. Forgiveness is the attribute of the strong."

We can be strong by emulating Jesus' example. He achieved our forgiveness in the most costly way possible – through His painful death on the cross.

If we confess our sins, He is faithful and just to forgive our sins and purify us from all unrighteousness. When we acknowledge our failures to Him, He will forgive and heal us.

With time and commitment we can create a lifestyle of forgiveness. This clears the way for a better future, one promising serenity and peace of mind.

God wants us to focus on the present and the future rather than the past. As Paul stated in Philippians 3: 13 -14, "No, dear brothers and sisters, I have not achieved it, but I focus on this one thing: Forgetting the past and looking forward to what lies ahead, I press on to reach the end of the race and receive the heavenly prize for which God, through Christ Jesus, is calling us."

It is pretty simple, really. If you want to experience contentment and joy, choose to forgive and be forgiven. Absolution is life-giving in ways that guilt, shame or anger never could be.

Forgiveness is the ultimate form of compassion. God notices every single time we choose to forgive. With regular practice, it can help us reach a blessed balance and equilibrium.

The story of Joseph in Genesis teaches us a lot about forgiveness. Time and again Joseph was treated unfairly, yet he never took his eyes off God. Joseph knew that God was in control. Because his faith never waivered, he could forgive at every juncture. This kind of attitude is what took him to the very top of leadership in Egypt.

When we forgive, we invite God into the situation. We are instructed in Scripture to forgive even the most ruthless enemy. Jesus gave us the perfect example of this. He trusted Himself completely to His Father. We can do no less if we wish to live a meaningful life.

Refusing to forgive is torment. It is inviting the devil into our lives. He wants to stir up anger, strife, hatred and bitterness. Rather, we should resolve to trust God with what we do not understand. Forgiving out of a sincere heart of love is downright healthy.

There are many strategies that can assist us with forgiveness. Writing about past painful experiences can be cathartic. Improving communication patterns can clear up basic misunderstandings. If pleasing God is your priority, you will choose to forgive every time.

Forgiveness takes courage. Ernest Hemingway stated that "courage is grace under pressure." If you and I are to act courageously, we must be very clear that our ultimate trust is in God.

David had a beautiful intimacy with the Lord. From his brave defeat of Goliath to his fearlessly honest expression of emotions in the Psalms, David was a stellar example of courage. His story gives us strength.

When the prophet Samuel told Jesse that one of his sons would be king, David was not even included in the lineup. That's how much David's family thought of him! But God will have his way. Samuel walked through the line of young men and asked if there were any more sons. Finally, David was called in from shepherding in the hills.

This should encourage us. God knows us. He sees us. He will not allow us to miss out on our destiny if we will trust Him in the same beautiful way that David did. Through his tending of sheep, God prepared David to shepherd the nation of Israel. Whatever it is you are doing, God can use it as a preparation for something great if you will only open your heart to His will.

David was steadfast in his refusal to disrespect King Saul, even after Samuel declared that David would be the next king. David honored Saul in every way though Saul mercilessly hunted him down. David had a wonderful friendship with Jonathan, Saul's son. And years after Saul and Jonathan were dead and gone, King David brought Jonathan's lame son, Mephibosheth, to his palace to live out the rest of his life.

God has a destiny for each of us if we are brave enough to reach out and take it. We must overcome our fears and claim our birthright. The answer to our deep seated anxieties is a vibrant, intimate relationship with Jesus Christ. He will respond with blessings and protection. Faith in Him allows courage to flow through every facet of our lives.

True courage is waiting on God and His timing. We must embrace the truth that God, in His infinite wisdom, will ultimately do what is best. When we don't know the answer, He is the answer.

Christ was perpetually courageous. He dealt with the most difficult of ordeals, and yet maintained patience, calm, and love to those who brutalized Him.

Like Christ, we can be diligent. We can refuse to give up, realizing that our mission is worth any price. When we believe in what we are doing, when the Lord's hand is upon us, we will be amazed at what we can accomplish.

We must have the courage necessary to take calculated risks. If we do not step out on a limb once in a while to do something important, we will fail to fulfill our mission. That would be tragic.

To produce good fruit, we must stay connected to Jesus, the Vine. We do this through studying the Bible and practicing prayer. When we are attached to the Vine, there will be joy…and Jesus will call us His friends. What better relationship could we have than to be friends with the living Christ?

He is our friend but He is also Divinity. He is no ordinary person. He deserves all the love and honor we can possibly give Him. With courage, we can achieve our ultimate purpose just as He designed.

It takes courage to persevere. Julie Andrews once said, "Perseverance is failing 19 times and succeeding the 20th." Perseverance means never giving up. It is staying the course until the end. It is taking the risk of responsibility and completing everything God would have you do.

As Martin Seligman pointed out, success comes from a combination of aptitude, motivation, and optimism. It is an attitude that says, with God's help – I can, you can, and we can.

Nehemiah had the vision and ability to set goals and achieve his purpose. He was able to accomplish an incredible feat – rebuilding the broken-down walls of Jerusalem in less than two months. He was passionate in his desire to create a safe and thriving city. God himself had said, "Jerusalem is the place in which I have chosen to live." (Nehemiah 1:9)

Like Nehemiah, if we are to persevere to the end, we must be prayer warriors. There were obstacles that greatly challenged Nehemiah. Sanballat and Tobiah badgered him. He created a plan for guarding the wall after it was rebuilt. He even devised a method to register all the people returning to Jerusalem with its newly secured borders.

His willingness to turn leadership over to Ezra when the need arose demonstrated just how mature Nehemiah really was. After a week of feasting, the Israelites fasted with sackcloth and ashes. Everything seemed to be in order, so Nehemiah returned to his old job in Persia.

But soon things in Jerusalem were once again in disarray. He returned immediately and ousted an enemy who had taken up sleeping quarters in the temple. He saw to it that the priests got paid fairly. He reminded everyone to keep the Sabbath holy. He reiterated to the Jewish people the importance of not marrying outside of their own race. Like Nehemiah, if we are following God's prompting with the heart of a servant, He will bless our efforts.

Our value is not based on how well we perform or the way other people view us. Our self-worth must rest firmly in God's love for us. He is our Creator. He is the one who is in ultimate control. We are here to fulfill His purposes, not our own. We must trust Him enough to persevere in the work He assigns us. We can have commitment and confidence even in the face of enormous trials.

Jesus was our ultimate example of perseverance. He went to the cross and paid the ultimate price so that you and I could be saved and receive eternal life. He went through horrendous suffering so that we could be together with Him forever.

In this book, we have explored the stories of Abraham's faith, Joshua and Caleb's optimism, Joseph's ability to forgive, David's courage, and Nehemiah's perseverance. Ultimately all stories will merge into His story – life everlasting spent glorifying Him. The choice is up to you – what will your story be?

ENDNOTES

Chapter 1

¹Michael Agnes, ed., *Webster's New World Dictionary* (New York: Pocket Books, 2003), 453.

Chapter 2

¹Rick Renner, *Sparkling Gems from the Greek* (Tulsa: OK: Teach All Nations, 2003), 65.

²Joel Osteen, "Become a Better You," as excerpted in *Enjoying Everyday Life Magazine*, January 2008, 24.

³Kenneth Pargament and Annette Mahoney, "Spirituality: Discovering and Conserving the Sacred," in *Handbook of Positive Psychology*, ed. C.R. Snyder and Shane Lopez, 646 -659 (USA, Oxford University Press, 2002), 646-7.

⁴Christopher Peterson and Nansook Park, "Classification and Measurement of Character Strengths: Implications for Practice," in *Positive Psychology in Practice*, ed. P. Alex Linley and Stephen Joseph, 433-446 (USA, Wiley, 2004), 438.

⁵Ibid.

⁶Pargament, 646.

⁷Ibid., 647

⁸Ibid., 648.

⁹Ibid., 648.

¹⁰William Bennett, *The Book of Virtues* (New York: Simon and Schuster, 1993), 741.

[11] David Meyers, "Human Connections and the Good Life: Balancing Individuality and Community in Public Policy," in *Positive Psychology in Practice*, 641-657 (see note 5) 642.

[12] Pargament, 648.

[13] Ibid., 650.

[14] Ibid., 651.

[15] Ibid., 651.

[16] Ibid., 653.

[17] Ibid., 655.

[18] Ibid., 655.

[19] R. Coles, *The Spiritual Lives of Children* (Boston: Houghton Mifflin, 1990), 141-2.

[20] Emily Dickenson, "I Never Saw a Moor," in *The Book of Virtues* (see note 11), 753.

[21] Pargament, 654.

Chapter 3

[1] Lisa Aspinwall and Ursula Staudinger, "A Psychology of Human Strengths; Some Central Issues of an Emerging Field," in *A Psychology of Human Strengths; Fundamental Questions and Future Directions for a Positive Psychology*, ed. Lisa Aspinwall and Ursula Staudnigner, 9-22 (Washington D.C., APA, 2003), 16.

[2] Ibid.

[3] Charles Carver and Michael Scheier, "Three Human Strengths" in *A Psychology of Human Strengths; Fundamental Questions and Future Directions for a Positive Psychology*, 87-102 (see note 1), 89.

[4]Penelope Green, "This is Your Brain on Happiness," *The Oprah Magazine* 9, no.3 (2008), 230.

[5]Gabrielle Leblanc, "5 Things Happy People Do," 233-235 (see note 4), 234.

[6]Ibid.

[7]Ibid., 235.

[8]Ibid., 235.

[9]Ibid., 235.

[10]C.W. Metcalf and Roma Felible, *Lighten Up: Survival Skills for People Under Pressure* (Cambridge, Massachusetts: Perseus Books, 1992), 6-7.

[11]*Google*, s.v. "Red Skelton quotes, thinkexist.com/quotation/live_by_this_credo_have_a_little_laugh_at_life/338308.html (accessed April 9, 2010).

[12]Martin Seligman, *Learned Optimism* (New York: Pocket Books, 1990), 10.

[13]Ibid., 16.

[14]Ibid., 208.

[15]Ibid., 173.s

[16]Daniel Gilbert, *Stumbling on Happiness* (New York; Alfred A. Knopf, 2006), 162.

[17]William James, *The Varieties of Religious Experience* (New York: New American Library, 1958), 107.

[18]*Google*, s.v. "Dietrich Bonhoeffer quotes," bonhoeffer/http://thinkexist.com/quotes/deitrich_2.html (Accessed April 9, 2010).

Chapter 4

[1] Martin Seligman, *Authentic Happiness: Using the New Positive Psychology to Realize Your Potential for Lasting Fulfillment* (New York: Free Press, 2002) 75.

[2] Ibid., 78.

[3] *Archaeological Study Bible, New International Version.* (Michigan: Zondervan, 2005), 67.

[4] Ibid., 3.

[5] Joyce Meyer, "Following Forgiveness instead of Emotions," *Enjoying Everyday Living* 22, no.5 (2008), 1.

[6] Ibid., 5.

[7] Ibid., 1.

[8] Ibid., 7.

[9] Ibid., 7.

[10] Joyce Meyer, *Conflict-free Living* (U.S.A.: Charisma House, 2008), 97.

[11] Ibid., 108.

[12] Frank Fincham and Todd Kashdan, "Facilitating Forgiveness: Developing Group and Community Interventions," in *Positive Psychology in Practice*, ed. P. Alex Linley and Stephen Joseph, 433-446 (USA, Wiley, 2004), 617.

[13] Ibid., 618.

[14] Ibid., 619.

[15] Ibid., 619-20.

[16] Ibid., 621-22.

[17] Ibid., 623.

[18]Ibid., 623.

[19]Ibid., 629.

[20]Ibid., 631.

Chapter 5

[1]Aristotle, *Nicomachean Ethics* as quoted in William Bennett, *The Book of Virtues* (New York: Simon and Schuster, 1993), 441.

[2]Beth Moore, *A Heart Like His: Intimate Reflections on the Life of David* (Nashville: Broadman and Holman, 2003), 11.

[3]Christopher Peterson and Nansook Park, "Classification and Measurement of Character Strengths: Implications for Practice," in *Positive Psychology in Practice*, ed. P. Alex Linley and Stephen Joseph, 433-446 (USA, Wiley, 2004), 437.

[4]Moore, 53.

[5]Peterson, 437.

[6]Moore, 59.

[7]Peterson, 437.

[8]Moore, 65.

[9]Ibid., 64.

[10]Dieter Frey, Eva Jonas, and Tobias Greitemeyer, "Intervention as a Major Tool of a Psychology of Human Strengths: Examples from Organizational Change and Innovation," in *A Psychology of Human Strengths: Fundamental Questions and Future Directions for a Positive Psychology*, ed. Lisa Aspinwall and Ursula Staudinger, 149-164 (Washington D.C., American Psychological Assocation, 2003),158.

[11]Ibid, 156.

[12] Moore, 81.

[13] Ibid., 103.

[14] Ibid., 169.

[15] Ibid., 108.

[16] Ibid., 109.

[17] Ibid., 114.

[18] Ibid., 120.

[19] Ibid., 122.

[20] Ibid., 170.

[21] Ibid., 177.

[22] Ibid., 178.

[23] Martin Seligman and Christopher Peterson, "Positive Clinical Psychology," in *A Psychology of Human Strengths*, 305- 317 (see note 6), 314.

[24] Moore, 199.

[25] Ibid., 206.

[26] Ibid., 214.

[27] Ibid., 224.

[28] Ibid., 256.

[29] Martin Seligman, *Authentic Happiness: Using the New Positive Psychology to Realize Your Potential for Lasting Fulfillment* (New York: Free Press, 2002), 145.

[30] Dan Baker and Cathy Greenberg, *What Happy Women Know: How New Findings in Positive Psychology Can Change Women's Lives for the Better* (USA: Rodale, 38-42.

[31] Seligman, *Authentic Happiness*, 146.

[32] Ibid., 147.

[33] "'Hurricane' Antigua Was a Pioneer for the Globetrotters," *The Cat's Pause*, August 2009, 5.

[34] "Remarkable Career Truly a Long Shot," *The Cat' Pause*, August 2009, 19.

[35] Tal Ben-Shahar, *Happier: Learn the Secrets to Daily Joy and Lasting Fulfillment* (New York: McGraw Hill, 2007), 100-101.

Chapter 6

[1] Martin Seligman, *Authentic Happiness: Using the New Positive Psychology to Realize Your Potential for Lasting Fulfillment* (New York: Free Press, 2002), 146.

[2] Martin Seligman, *Learned Optimism* (New York: Pocket Books, 1990), 101.

[3] Ibid.

[4] John Maxwell, *The 21 Indispensable Qualities of a Leader: Becoming the Person Others Will Want to Follow* (Nashville: Thomas Nelson, 1999), xi.

[5] Seligman, *Authentic Happiness*, 182.

[6] Jeanne Nakamura and Mihaly Csikszentmihalyi, "The Concept of Flow," in *Handbook of Positive Psychology*, ed. C.R. Snyder and Shane Lopez, 89-105 (USA, Oxford, 2002), 95-6.

[7] Charles Swindoll, *Hand Me Another Brick* (New York: Bantam Books, 1986), 17.

[8] Ibid., 13.

[9] Ibid., 9.

[10] Robert Emmons, "Personal Goals, Life Meaning, and Virtue: Wellspring of a Positive Life," in *Flourishing: Positive Psychology and the Life*

Well-Lived, ed. Corey Keyes and Jonathan Haidt, 105-128 (Washington DC, APA, 2003) 123.

[11]Swindoll, 20.

[12]Ibid, 26.

[13]Ibid, 29.

[14]Ibid, 33.

[15]Seligman, *Learned Optimism*, 255.

[16]Seligman, *Authentic Happiness*, 246.

[17]Swindoll, 3.

[18]Vic Johnson, "Simply Solving the Puzzle," *Your Achievement E-zine* 327 (2007) www.ezine@yoursuccessstore.com (accessed September 5, 2007).

[19]Seligman, *Learned Optimism*, 104.

[20]Swindoll, 84.

[21]Ibid., 107.

[22]Ibid., 106.

[23]Martin Seligman, "Positive Psychology, Positive Prevention, and Positive Therapy," in *Handbook of Positive Psychology*, 3-9 (see note 6), 3.

[24]Swindoll, p.113.

[25]Nakamura, 93.

[26]Ken.Blanchard and Phil Hodges, *The Servant Leader: Transforming Your Heart, Head, Hands and Habits* (Nashville: Countryman, 2003) 49.

[27]Charles Carver and Michael Scheier, "Three Human Strengths" in *A Psychology of Human Strengths: Fundamental Questions and Future Directions for a*

Positive Psychology ed. Lisa Aspinwall and Ursula Staudinger, 87-102 (Washington DC, APA, 2003) 88.

[28]Ibid., 89.

[29]Joyce Meyer, *A Leader in the Making: Essentials to Being a Leader After God's Own Heart* (Tulsa: Harrison House, 2001), 245.

ABOUT THE AUTHOR

Kimberly Mittendorf Hensley is a Christian writer and life coach for people with disabilities and their caregivers.

She is a licensed professional counselor with Master's degrees in community counseling and the education of people with disabilities. She has received certificates in Christian life coaching through Light University and the American Association of Christian Counselors (AACC). She has completed 87 hours of training in life coaching. She has also completed 27 modules from the AACC on *The Blessing Project: Creating a Culture of Blessing in Your Home and with Others*.

She has completed studies in Shakespeare, The Art of Public Speaking, The Art of Teaching, Positive Psychology, and the Old and New Testaments. She is a graduate of the Jerry B. Jenkins Christian Writer's Guide Journeyman Program.

While working at Clermont Counseling Center from 1997 – 2005, she gave over forty speeches at various conferences and meetings. She created and implemented a consumer medication education curriculum. She also created and implemented a positive psychology program entitled, *Claim Your Strengths; Reclaim Your Life*.

Kimberly published her nonfiction book, *Aptitudes for Growth; Attitudes for Success*, in 2010. She has reworked the material from the book into four mini-books. Those updated mini- books will be: *Applying Inspiring Biographies from the Bible for Personal Growth: Examining Faith, Optimism, Forgiveness, Courage, and Perseverance (Book One)*, *Applying Inspiring Biographies from the Bible for Personal Growth: Examining Patience, Wisdom, Peace, Enthusiasm and Commitment, Gratitude and Happiness (Book Two)*, *Friendship: The Heartbeat of Love*, and *Our Wonderful Three-in-One God*.

Also in process is a mini-book entitled, *Enjoying Reading: Think, Learn, and Grow for a Lifetime*. She is working hard as well on a full-length non-fiction book, *Everybody Has Needs: A Positive Christian Approach for People with Disabilities and Their Caregivers*.

Kimberly was selected as the Outstanding Graduate of the University of Cincinnati's Community Counseling Program in 2002. She received the Wasserman Champion Award from the Clermont Mental Health and Recovery Board in 2003.

Dear reader,

You would help me greatly by reviewing this book on Amazon.com. Thank you for your support.

I would love to hear from you. My email address is khensley@zoomtown.com. My website is www.supportbykim.com which also promotes my Christian coaching business for people with disabilities and their caregivers.

My next book will be available soon. It is titled, *Applying Inspiring Biographies from the Bible for Personal Growth: Examining Patience, Wisdom, Peace, Enthusiasm and Commitment, Gratitude, and Happiness (Book Two)*. I hope you will check it out.

Blessings,

Kimberly

Made in the USA
Charleston, SC
18 December 2015